THE NEW TIMES NETWORK

THE NEW TIMES NETWORK

GROUPS AND CENTRES FOR PERSONAL GROWTH

COMPILED BY
ROBERT ADAMS

WITH A FOREWORD BY
DAVID SPANGLER

ROUTLEDGE & KEGAN PAUL
LONDON, BOSTON, MELBOURNE
AND HENLEY

First published in 1982
by Routledge & Kegan Paul Ltd
39 Store Street, London WC1E 7DD,
9 Park Street, Boston, Mass. 02108, USA,
296 Beaconsfield Parade, Middle Park,
Melbourne, 3206, Australia, and
Broadway House, Newtown Road,
Henley-on-Thames, Oxon RG9 1EN
Set in Times by
Input Typesetting Ltd, London
and printed in Great Britain by
The Thetford Press Ltd
Thetford, Norfolk

Library of Congress Cataloging in Publication Data

The new times network.
Bibliography: p.
1. Group relations training – Directories.
2. Communal living – Directories.   3. Utopias.
I. Adams, Robert, 1958–
HM133.N487   1983   303.4'9   82–13207

ISBN 0-7100-9355-1

Try not to focus on the outer manifestation of groups and individuals but see the Plan as a whole – each having its place and allotted role to play.

Lodge of the Star

CONTENTS

FOREWORD
OLD VOYAGE, NEW VOYAGERS: THE MATURING OF
PLANETARY CULTURE BY DAVID SPANGLER   vii

PREFACE   xiii

ACKNOWLEDGMENTS   xv

HOW TO USE THE DIRECTORY   xvii

1 **HEALTH AND HEALING**   1
INTRODUCTION BY HAROLD WICKS

2 **GROWTH AND HUMAN POTENTIAL**   29
INTRODUCTION BY SABINE KURJO

3 **HOLISTIC EDUCATION**   55
INTRODUCTION BY GEOFFREY LEYTHAM

4 **SPIRITUAL TRADITIONS**   71
INTRODUCTION BY WINIFRED BREWIN

5 **NEW AGE COMMUNITIES**   97
INTRODUCTION BY FRANÇOIS DUQUESNE

CONTENTS

6 NETWORKS, ASSOCIATIONS, INFORMATION CENTRES   111
INTRODUCTION BY SIR JOHN SINCLAIR

7 MAGAZINES AND JOURNALS   129

8 CONCLUSION   142
THE NEW PILGRIMAGE BY SIR GEORGE TREVELYAN

FOREWORD

OLD VOYAGE, NEW VOYAGERS: THE MATURING OF PLANETARY CULTURE
BY DAVID SPANGLER

This directory testifies to the existence of a little recognized, little understood but important force in human affairs. This is the force of the idea of a new age, an image of transformation and the emergence of a new human culture. At a time when the tensions and conflicts between East and West, rich and poor, humanity and nature seem to preclude any hope for a constructive and harmonious future, the idea of a new age proclaims that the final hand has not yet been dealt on behalf of our human destiny; we still have some aces up the collective sleeve of our spirit and creativity.

There are three basic visions of the future motivating people in the world today. One is the vision that somehow we will muddle through the various crises and challenges besetting humanity, perhaps with the aid of new technologies, and that the future will be a continuation of the present; we will survive and continue on our course. The second is that we will not muddle through, that the tensions and problems will overwhelm us in their complexity and intensity, and civilization will collapse, perhaps in the white heat of a nuclear embrace, perhaps in the slower death of ecological disruption and a declining quality of life. The third is that what we are experiencing now are not the harbingers of death but the pangs of a birth and that out of the turmoil of the present decades a new expression of culture will emerge, transforming our future and setting us on a new pathway of the human adventure.

The chances that this third vision will triumph do not seem hopeful if one views the world through the lens of our daily media. Our newspapers, news magazines and television programs act as a kind of primitive nervous system oriented generally to perceiving events that are either threats or emotionally stimulating. They suffer from a kind of evolutionary myopia, unable to see a larger context of growth and change in the world around them. If one looks beyond the range of the media, though, and examines some of the activities represented in this book, a different perspective emerges. One becomes aware of the wide range of efforts and innovative developments springing from a vision of world transformation and creativity. Then, this third vision of our future does not seem quite so far-fetched.

In fact, the idea of the new age is rooted in one of the oldest human images, that of the holy (or holistic) human civilization. This image, sometimes called the New Jerusalem, the City of God, or, in the Orient, Shamballa, is one of a human culture in full harmony and attunement within itself, with nature, and with God: a culture in which the divine perspective of love and wholeness can find full expression.

The desire for such a civilization has empowered human striving and efforts throughout our history, particularly here in the West. It has been the impetus behind numerous millennial movements and eschatological expectations. It has been the imagination behind the idea of utopia. The quest for such a perfected civilization is indeed an old voyage, however much the present new age subculture may proclaim its revolutionary and 'new' status in the history of human ideas and activities.

To me, this voyage has a meaning beyond the quest for a benign, secure, efficient civilization, a land of peace and harmony. It is a voyage to understand ourselves; it is a voyage of maturation. The image of the new age or of the planetary culture is much more than an image of culture. It speaks of a state of being, a level of conscious connectedness and skillfully harmonious interaction between humankind and the whole web of life in which our interests and its interests become mutually empowering or synergistic. Just as when a person matures, he or she comes to realize that his or her wellbeing is closely tied up with the wellbeing of others, so it is with our species. There is an aspect of our humanness, our essential identity, and a portion of our power as creative beings that will only become accessible to us when we are accessible in a loving and caring fashion with the rest of our world.

There is an image that is often referred to amongst the people and groups with whom I most often work, and that is the image of the 'earth community'. By this, no particular place or group of people is meant. Rather, the image implies a state of communion between all the lives that make up our global ecological family. Yet, in one way, this community has always existed. It is not a new appearance. What is happening now is that humanity is learning how to be skillfully and consciously a participant in this community in ways that can benefit ourselves and this larger whole. It is the emergence of our conscious citizenship in the earth community that most closely reflects, I feel, the meaning of the idea of a new age.

This emergence is not through traditional forms of social change, for it is primarily a shift of consciousness, an expansion of awareness, a deepening and broadening of our sensitivity. Its tools are inner exploration along appropriate lines, demonstration, identification and resonance. We see these tools represented by the groups and activities listed in this directory.

Since part of this emergence is developing an expanded way of looking at our world, there is a need for inner, personal work, the kind of self-examination that can enlarge our perceptions of our planetary identity. This is more than the tendency towards self-absorption sometimes found in the more narcissistic elements of the human potential movement. It is the quest to discover the self we can share with others in ways that are mutually uplifting and empowering. This is the self that gives in order that a larger wholeness can be enhanced, knowing that within that enhancement, the context of its own being and growth is equally enlarged.

Thus, the inner quest is balanced by an outer demonstration, a kind of laboratory of action in which our expanding, maturing perceptions of wholeness can be put to the test in human relationship. Centers of demonstration help us sort out our skills and provide an opportunity to see how our ideas of a new culture, a new age, work out in practice. When they do work, they provide a message to the world at large, a message of hope potentially more powerful than any media fascination with the dimensions of hopelessness.

The third tool is identification. In the past, when the image of a planetary culture or a holy culture has emerged in human affairs, it has become the rallying cry of a particular group of visionaries and revolutionaries against other groups of people attached to the status quo. It has acted as a sword between people, as an ideology or a belief that separates and generates conflict. However, we cannot know who we are as mature human beings when we are separated from our fellows. If the image of the earth community or the planetary culture has any meaning at all, it lies in its ability to help us have a context of human development and worth embracing all people, even those who cannot share that perspective with us. In short, the new age idea cannot be another ideology separating us into believers and non-believers. Rather it lives in us to the degree it empowers our capacity to communicate, to understand, to touch each other and to share the essence of community.

Finally, the fourth tool of emergence is resonance. This is the power of an idea to strike a chord of familiarity and meaning within us so that it becomes part of us, a power that is enhanced as it strikes an increasing number of chords in a growing number of people. It is communication beyond words, beyond thought, even. It is the sharing of an identity of growth transcending, yet honoring, our differences. It is a state of attunement to each other and to our world so that the efforts we make and the effects of our activities support and empower the efforts and lives of others . . . including those others within nature who are not human as we are but who nevertheless share the overall instincts of life and unfoldment.

All of the activities and efforts described in this book represent these tools at work. They are not so much activities of transformation as they are embodied signs of a maturation process within our species. After all, a child matures when faced with adult challenges; so we are maturing to face and resolve planetary challenges transcending our experiences as regional, ethnic and parochial beings.

The power of the New Age Movement, as represented by the efforts listed herein, is not a power only of social persuasion. It is a power aligned with the natural instincts of growth within our species, currently struggling with a certain fascination with death and destruction. There is in us a desire to discover our true power and identity and a deep intuition that we will only do so in a holistic, planetary context in which we become sources of power for the wholeness of global unfoldment. The New Age Movement aligns with that desire and that intuition and draws its power from them.

This power is at work in our world. If anyone wishes to be convinced of this, then this directory gives specific places to begin an exploration. In undertaking such a search, that person becomes a new voyager upon an old voyage, the voyage of human maturation into a truly planetary species. It is a voyage that is about to take on a new meaning and a new thrust, and we are privileged to be offered the opportunity of participation at a time when this quest honors its history by empowering us to revision and recreate our future.

PREFACE

The first half of the twentieth century saw the consummation of the industrial age. Today we are living in the post-industrial era, called by many the age of communication – expressed through modern media and space and air travel. The computer, the television and the telephone have brought the world to our doorsteps and encouraged that sense of recognition that we are one humanity living on one planet. The problems of the world are the problems of all men. The constant availability and circulation of information has and still is increasing our global responsibilities in all directions. This rapidly expanding field of human communications is one of the key factors behind the revolution taking place in human consciousness and the growth in awareness of the spiritual nature of man and the universe.

Today individuals and groups exist everywhere who are encouraging others to move into a new mode of living. We see before us a vast panorama of alternative lifestyles exemplified in community living, new therapies for mind and body, techniques to aid self-awareness and much more. Through easy availability of information many people can explore positively the creative ways of enhancing their own evolution.

This point of time has been foretold by mystics down the ages as a time of transition into a new age when a cross-over point in evolution will be reached. Groups everywhere and in many ways are actively involved in this transitional period. At one time only the few could be reached, but now due to our global communications system all can be reached and inspired by the onrush of new ideas and qualities of living.

The New Age, generally speaking, is simply the attainment by mankind of a higher level of consciousness. Over the ages man has emerged from a purely instinctive nature into an intuitive state of being which is destined to be expressed fully in the New Age. Man has grown more responsive to the needs of others and has become more attuned to the higher spiritual realities.

This book is an attempt to show these realities working out in the teachings and practices of the many groups operating around the world and is very much a part of today's growing communications field. A book of this kind can never be complete but should be found representative as it serves as a doorway to a whole new world of reality. Its usefullness will be proved in differing ways – the general reader will be faced with a movement of new values to explore, and the seeker will be able to select those techniques through which he feels his pathway lies. Have a fruitful journey.

ROBERT ADAMS

ACKNOWLEDGMENTS

I would like to thank all those who have helped with this work. Special thanks are due to all the contributors, John Sinclair for his help and advice, Eileen Wood for her support, Steven Barron for the initial mailout, my parents for their efforts and all those others for their inspiration in preparing this guide.

HOW TO USE
THE DIRECTORY

The reader will find that the process of extracting information from this book is straightforward. The directory, as will be seen from the contents page, is divided into a number of different sections each headed by an introduction from a prominent thinker. Following this introduction each section has been divided into geographical regions consisting of the United Kingdom, North America, Europe and the rest of the world. The groups are alphabetically listed within each region. This enables information to be retrieved with some ease. The details published about each group give a clear description of activity, programmes and publications. Further information can be obtained direct from the organization.

NOTE

The material contained in this directory has been classified in accordance with indications given by the various groups. It should be borne in mind that these classifications are only general and are there to aid the reader. Many groups could be included under other sections and some under all sections. Most groups can provide information on their field areas and many are prepared to share their resources with other groups. Readers are asked to enquire for these facilities. Most group leaders are also prepared to lecture to others; again, enquiries should be made.

1

HEALTH AND HEALING

INTRODUCTION
BY HAROLD WICKS

A curious phenomena of our scientific age has been the rapidly increasing level of public interest in methods of healing and health maintenance that for many years had been discarded by scientific orthodoxy.

Dominant twentieth-century allopathic techniques rely in the main upon physical chemical methods of immunology, surgery and the destruction of invading organisms by drugs. Although there is no doubt as to the achievements of allopathy in the control of certain acute conditions and infectious diseases, it is also true to say that they have left some problems unsolved and appear to have created others. On a broad basis, worries are being expressed about the conservatism of modern medical practice and about the side-effects of some therapeutic and diagnostic techniques.

In many western countries there is also growing unease with the rapidly increasing costs of providing adequate medical services and associated social services, while at an international level there is substantial concern as to the suitability of some modern medical techniques for use in developing countries. It was because of these worries that in 1978 the World Health Organization, at a major conference at Alma Ata, committed itself to a programme of primary health care depending upon the appropriate use of both traditional and Western methods.

Parallel with these changes of attitude, there has been a rising

3

level of public and medical interest in what used to be called Fringe Medicine, which during the 1970s was termed Alternative Medicine and which is now becoming established as Complementary Medicine. In general, this term now refers to a style of medicine that attempts to deal with health and disease in terms of the whole organism – mind, emotions, body and spirit – rather than concentrating on particular symptoms and their immediate causes. In disease the patient's own healing processes are helped, and in health individual responsibility is encouraged in terms of behaviour and lifestyle.

In this section of the Directory, the reader will find reference to a multitude of Complementary Therapies, associations of therapists, treatment centres and information networks. These, together with the quantity of available literature, the dramatic increase in self-treatment by herbal and health products and the increasing space given to the subject by the media, are all evidence of the growth of this interest in gentle, non-invasive methods of treatment.

One paradox of this revival of the older therapies is the constant appearance of what seem to be new therapeutic techniques. In addition to the 'classical', well-structured systems such as acupuncture, chiropractic, homoeopathy, medical herbalism and osteopathy, the public finds itself faced with a great variety of lesser known techniques. Some lay heavy emphasis on diet and lifestyle, others concentrate upon counselling and techniques of psychotherapy which themselves can be based upon either Western psychology or Eastern spiritual systems – or both; there are postural, manipulative and massage therapies and yet others based on dance, art and music, plus, of course, the very important section which includes healing.

But it is only a paradox because what in fact we see is a range of therapies – new, old and variations on the old – which all start from the same holistic standpoint; they have in common their understanding of the importance of the organism as a whole but they give varying emphasis to different aspects of it. Some emphasize physical inputs and physical reactions, some concentrate on mental control of physical functions, others focus on the development of consciousness, and so on. Probably no one is in itself a complete system and suitable to every circumstance. The therapies and techniques are indeed complementary, both to each other and to modern allopathic specialities. Thus, the term Complementary Medicine is right because it points to the correct relationship that should exist between all therapies – that of co-operation, understanding and appropriate application.

4

It was this realization that directed the Healing Research Trust to found the Institute for Complementary Medicine, a body that would provide a neutral ground upon which therapy organizations could meet and co-ordinate and learn about each other, where the processes of negotiation with national and local professional bodies could take place and where, through the Information and Documentation Centre, sound and reliable data could be made available to all interested parties.

Note Harold Wicks is a Director of the Threshold Foundation and of the London based Institute for Complementary Medicine. Threshold has conceived and funded a survey into the status of Complementary Medicine in the UK which will form the starting point for continuing scientific research into this field. It is also the basis of the Institute's Public Information and Documentation Centre.

UK

AQUARIAN HEALING TRUST
(Gerry Martin, Warden)
1 Claremont Avenue
Woking, Surrey GU 22 7SF
☎ 048 62 66510

The Trust offers spiritual healing, counselling and meditation, free of charge. Training programmes are run in meditation and healing. There is a meeting room and counselling room open for others of like mind to visit. The Warden and his wife visit and address groups on healing and counselling.

BATH YOGA CENTRE
(Paul Harvey, Director)
11 Rowacres
Bath BA2 2LH
☎ 0225 26327

Bath Yoga Centre offers group and individual classes focusing on yoga tuition and yoga therapy. The teaching is in the tradition of Professor T. Krishnamachakya and his son T. K. V. Desikachar. Classes are available on philosophy, postures, breathing and therapy. The Director is able to give talks and advice on all aspects of yoga outside the Centre.

THE BAYLY SCHOOL OF REFLEXOLOGY
(Nicola M. Hall, Principal)
Monks Orchard
Whitbourne, Worcester WR6 5RB
☎ 0886 21207

Reflexology is a form of ancient Chinese medicine involving treatment through massage of pressure points in the feet. It can be helpful to many disorders and is also a relaxing therapy.

The Bayly School holds courses leading to a Certificate in London and some Certificate courses may be held outside London in the future. In addition, courses are held in Holland and Switzerland. General introductory talks and courses are held around the country.

The School has a list of Reflexology practitioners and treatment from the principal is available at the above address and in Cheltenham.

Books and charts on Reflexology are also available.

BRITISH WHEEL OF YOGA
(Pat Chittananda, General Secretary)
'Sivananda'
Pies Cottages, Pies Farm
Farringdon, Nr Alton, Hants GU34 3ET

The British Wheel of Yoga is a registered charity whose purpose is 'to help all persons to a greater knowledge and understanding of all aspects of yoga and its practice, by the provision of facilities for research, study, education and training', and which desires 'to cooperate with and support other organizations having similar objectives'. The Wheel has a membership of approximately 4,000, many of whom are available for seminars and workshops; there is a Teacher's Diploma, the syllabus for which is available on request.

Publications: 'Spectrum', quarterly magazine for members; 'Start Living with Yoga', Phillip Jones; 'Yoga Handbook'; 'Yoga Poetry'; 'Karma Yoga', Jean Herbert; 'How to use the *Bhagavad Gita*', Jean Herbert; *Tape* 'An Introduction to Sanskrit'.

THE CENTRE FOR ARCANE MEDICINE & HEALING
(Francesca Rossetti, DD)
6 Ruscombe Close, Southborough
Nr Tunbridge Wells, Kent TN4 0SG
☎ 0892 30142

The 'whole person' is treated at the Centre, the spiritual level being the most important; also offered are self-healing, cosmic education, diet, and an advisory service. The Centre specializes in radionics, herbs, colour therapy, Dr Bach remedies and spiritual healing. Seminars are held in London and Tunbridge Wells, public lectures at Caxton Hall. Training programmes are run in many aspects of natural healing and education on an esoteric level. Information is available on psychic health and healing.

Publication: Booklet, 'Psychic Health Research'.

CENTRE FOR HEALING & SPIRITUAL UNDERSTANDING
(Beverley Milne, Director)
49 The Avenue
London, NW6
☎ 01 459 0764

Spiritual science teaching and inner growth workshops include Living Meditation, Intuitive Foot Massage (Certificate), Self-help Foot Massage, Breathing/Movement for Relaxation, Spiritual Law, Colour Healing,

Psychic Self-protection, 'I Ching', etc. There are visiting speakers on natural therapies.

The Centre has a wholefood vegetarian orientation. There is a library and personal services of guidance, healing, relaxation therapy, t'ai-chi tuition, and a training programme for inner growth are available. A meeting/meditation room is open to the public. Referral to therapists and healers is available, as is spiritually oriented (holistic) advice on healing, life direction, psychological and marriage problems.

Publication: Newsletter each term. 'Spiritual Teaching for the New Age', by The Teacher.

THE COMMUNITY HEALTH FOUNDATION
188 Old Street
London, EC1
☎ 01 251 4076

The Community Health Foundation is concerned with preventive medicine and through its East-West Centre public classes provides simple, practical techniques for self-help health care. There is a health consultancy service, a nursery school, the Seven Sheaves macrobiotic restaurant; and the Kushi Institute for intensive study of shiatsu massage, for teachers and health counsellors. Speakers are available on health, diet, nutrition, oriental diagnosis, macrobiotic cooking and shiatsu massage.

Publications: 'East-West Centre Newsletter' (bi-monthly); 'Kushi Institute Journal' (quarterly).

COTSWOLD NATURAL HEALTH CENTRE
51 Rodney Road
Cheltenham, Glos. GL50 1HR
☎ 0242 25437

The Centre exists to promote an understanding of alternative medicine, to encourage therapists to work together and to encourage members of the public to take a greater responsibility for their own health. Courses and lectures are open to the public in all aspects of health care, along with extensive therapy treatment service including acupuncture, osteopathy, naturopathy, homeopathy, healing, herbalism, massage, etc. Short training programmes in the above and in aspects of health care are offered. A meeting room is available to outside groups, and speakers are available to lecture on all aspects of health care, with particular emphasis on areas where individuals can learn simple techniques to maintain their own health, through diet, exercise, meditation, etc.

Publication: Newsletter – quarterly.

DELAWARR LABORATORIES LTD

Raleigh Park Road
Oxford, OX2 9BB
☎ 0865 48572

Delawarr Laboratories operate a service for advice, diagnosis and therapy using radionic instruments available all over the world. Instruments made by the Laboratories are also for sale, with training in their use. Leonard P. Corte, Director, is available to lecture on radionic concepts. Information is also available on subjects concerned with alternative medicine and parapsychology.

Publication: Information Service Newsletter, quarterly, on subscription.

THE DR BACH CENTRE

Mount Vernon, Sotwell
Wallingford, Oxon., OX10 0PZ
☎ 0491 39489

The healing of dis-ease and disharmony through the personality by the means of wild flowers discovered by Edward Bach, MB, BS, MRCS, LRCP, DPH. Treat the person – and not the physical complaint – the cause not the effect. The specialized services of the Centre are the supply of remedies, advice, recommendation and information on Bach remedies.

Publications: 'The Twelve Healers'; 'Heal Thyself'; 'Handbook A.B.F.R.'; 'Medical Discoveries'; 'Dictionary Illustrated'.

GEDDES POSITIVE HEALTH ASSOCIATES

89 Woodfield Road
Thames Ditton, Surrey, KT7 0DS
☎ 01 398 4556

Alec Geddes ia a practising healer for the National Federation of Spiritual Healers, and also does reflexology and massage, and gives diet advice. Sheila Geddes is a professional astrologer who runs the Geddes Astrological College, teaching astrology and astrological counselling by means of tape cassettes. They offer lectures on alternative medicine and demonstrations of reflexology. Information is normally only offered to patients on an individual basis.

THE GLOSSOP CENTRE

(Mrs Ronnie Williams)
3 Spinney Close
Glossop, Derbs SK13 9BR
☏ 04574 3563

Mrs Williams runs a branch of the Atlanteans, a meditation group, and has links with other New Age groups in the N. Derbyshire and Manchester area. A series of lectures is organized each autumn, covering alternative medicine, healing and New Age philosophy; occasional weekend courses and one-day seminars are also run. Mrs Williams specializes in meditation and healing, and offers information on spiritual growth. She is able to give talks on herbs and herbalism, alternative medicine and holistic healing. She can put people in touch with local and regional practitioners, teachers and speakers of alternative therapies, including reflexology, massage, yoga, etc.

THE HEALING CENTRE

Warren Hill Farmhouse
Trunch, North Walsham, Norfolk
☏ 026 379 493

The Centre offers absent and contact healing, counselling and information on alternative therapies and cancer help centres. They have contact with a cancer therapy group at Diss. Training is available for those interested in becoming healers. Barbara Neale is available to speak on healing and the philosophy of living.

HEALTH FOR THE NEW AGE

1a Addison Crescent
London W14 8JP
☏ 01 603 7751

Health for the New Age has been run by Marcus McCausland since 1972 and has since then been investigating new approaches to positive health care, and acting as consultants on all aspects of health and ill health. It has sponsored many programmes on holistic health and through its activities has brought together many professionals concerned with these fields.

At the same address is the Association for New Approaches to Cancer. The association provides information to the public and health care professionals about complementary approaches to cancer diagnosis, therapies and prevention, with particular emphasis on the holistic approach. The association sponsors several conferences and courses.

Publication: 'Health for the New Age' newsletter.

HOLISTIC HEALTH, BIOFEEDBACK & MEDITATION COURSES, AUDIO LTD

26 Wendell Road
London, W12 9RT
☎ 01 743 1518

Biofeedback, relaxation training and meditation are available both to the general public and as training courses.

Publication: 'The Awakened Mind', by C. M. Cade and Nona Coxhead (Wildwood House).

HYGEIA STUDIOS

Colour-Light-Art Research Ltd
Brook House
Avening, Tetbury, GL8 8NS
☎ 045 383 2150

Hygeia Studios offers colour therapy and an environmental design service. Courses are available on colour therapy.

Publication: 'The Colour Circle'.

THE INSTITUTE FOR COMPLEMENTARY MEDICINE

21 Portland Place
London W1N 3AF
☎ 01 636 9543

The Institute marks a big step forward in the establishment of alternative health treatments. Founded by the Healing Research Trust, under the chairmanship of Major General Sir Digby Raeburn, the Institute aims to promote the interests of all suitably qualified practitioners and seeks to unite the efforts of all who share their objectives.

The Institute will be organizing public lectures, classes and courses in its own building and elsewhere, in co-operation with organized groups, local authorities and other appropriate associations. It also maintains a public information and documentation centre covering many aspects of complementary medicine relevant to practitioners, patients and researchers. The Institute administers the provincial information points (PIPs). A national network of PIPs is being developed to provide local information about complementary medicine, organize discussion groups and run adult education classes in co-operation with local authorities when this is possible. The Institute will also administer the Association for Complementary Medicine, members will receive information about complementary therapies and will be kept informed of the Institute's work through regular newsletters. Subscription income will be used to support the Institute.

Holistic treatments are now receiving a great deal of support, dealing as they do with the whole person – body, mind and spirit. The Institute for Complementary Medicine is increasing this support and is one of the most important developments to date in this field.

THE INTERNATIONAL ASSOCIATION OF COLOUR HEALERS

(Mrs W. Kent)
33 St Leonards Court, St Leonards Road
East Sheen, London, SW14 7NG
☎ 01 876 5225

The Association explores all areas of colour healing and is also involved in magnetic healing and alternative medicine research. Workshops are conducted on healing and psychic development.

Publication: Newsletter.

KESTEVEN NATURAL HEALTH CENTRE

(Sue and Harry Fuller)
Church Farm, Great Hale
Sleaford, Lincs
☎ 0529 60536

The Kesteven Natural Health Trust has been formed to assist the Centre, which offers teaching, seminars, forums, and treatment and information on natural therapies. Training is available at the Centre in first-aid homeopathy, Bach remedies, acupressure and massage. Speakers are available on the above subjects and biochemics.

Publication: Newsletter to Trust members.

LONDON & COUNTIES SOCIETY OF PHYSIOLOGISTS

100 Waterloo Road
Blackpool, Lancs, FY4 1AW
☎ 0253 403548

This is a professional body representing therapists in massage, manipulative therapy, osteopathy, health and beauty therapy, and allied therapies, with a membership in excess of 1200.

Publication: Annual list of members and Directory of practitioners.

THE MAITREYA SCHOOL OF HEALING
(R. H. Leech)
7 Penland Road
Bexhill on Sea, E. Sussex
☎ 0424 211450

The School both offers and teaches healing by mental colour therapy. Mr Leech and Miss L. R. Cornford (26 Lyndhurst Gardens, London, NW3) lecture on mental colour therapy and associated subjects.

There are also centres in London, Birmingham, Worcester and Brighton, which are open to potential students, and to the general public who wish to attend lectures or receive counselling.

Publication: Quarterly newsletter.

NATIONAL FEDERATION OF SPIRITUAL HEALERS
Old Manor Farm Studio
Church Street
Sunbury on Thames
Middlesex, TW16 6RG
☎ 093 27 83164

The Federation was founded as the expression of a pressing need to establish a national body which would co-ordinate, protect and advance the work of spiritual healing. It registers as healer members those accepted for membership who produce authenticated evidence of spiritual healing acceptable to a panel of Federation executives. The Federation which encourages full healing potential also runs a service open to the public seeking spiritual healing by putting them in touch with approved members of the federation.

Publication: Journal – 'Healing Review'.

NATURAL HEALTH NETWORK
51 Rodney Road
Cheltenham, Glos, GL50 1HX
☎ 0242 25437

The Network's function is to link together natural health centres, and individuals who wish to promote holistic health care, both for existing natural health centres and individuals who wish to start one. Courses are offered on how to set up and run a natural health centre. Information is available on natural health centres, 20 of which are members of the Network, which also has 1000 individual members.

Publication: 'Keys', available to members.

THE NATURECARE CENTRE
300 Streatham High Road
Streatham, London SW16
☎ 01 274 8534

The Centre is one for holistic medicine, offering treatment, advice and training courses. Holistic medicine is seen to include acupuncture, aromatherapy, herbalism, homeopathy, hypnotherapy, iridology, osteopathy, psychotherapy, rebirthing, reflexology, nutrition. Speakers are available to talk on holistic therapies.

Publication: Newsletter.

NORTHERN INSTITUTE OF MASSAGE
100 Waterloo Road
Blackpool, Lancs, FY4 1AW
☎ 0253 403548

The Institute offers training services in massage, manipulative therapy, health and beauty therapy, and allied therapies.

Publications: Various course texts and tutorial manuals; 'Skill Bulletin'.

ORGANIC LIVING ASSOCIATION
(Dennis C. Nightingale-Smith, Director/Secretary)
St Mary's Villa
Hanley Swan, Worcester, WR8 0EA

The aims of the Association are to promote good health, good nutrition, organic growing, ecology and ecological villages by organizing conferences, festivals, visits and education.

Publication: Newsletter.

THE RADIONIC ASSOCIATION LIMITED
(Miss Anita J. Dunn, Secretary)
16a North Bar
Banbury, Oxon, OX16 0TF
☎ 0295 3183

The Radionic Association, founded in 1943, is the professional society of qualified radionic practitioners (Fellows, Members, Licentiates). It is also a society of lay members (Associates). Its conferences and general meetings are open to the public. Training is offered by the Association's School of Radionics. There is a list available of official speakers on radionics.

Publication: 'Radionic Quarterly', journal published March, June, September and December.

SCHOOL OF HERBAL MEDICINE

148 Forest Road,
Tunbridge Wells, Kent, TN2 5EY
☎ 0892 30400

The School offers three courses on herbal medicine: four-year, full-time; four-year tutorial (correspondence) and one-year (correspondence). Speakers are available on application to the School, and they also offer information on herbal treatment, practitioners and firms supplying herbs.

Publication: List of herbal practitioners.

SCHOOL OF T'AI-CHI CH'UAN

(Beverley Milne, Director)
82a Chiltern Street,
London, W1
Office: 49 The Avenue,
London, NW6
☎ 01 459 0764

Holistic training in this callisthenic healing art of movement meditation, Long Form with variations. Sensitive guidance in body alignment, relaxation, integrated breathing/movement, applied meditation, symbolism, energy dynamics, spiritual science, 'I Ching' and Chinese philosophy related to Western and the One Life. Additional studies through associated Centre for Healing, and library.

Publication: 'T'ai-Chi spirit and essence', Beverley Milne.

THE SEEKERS TRUST

(Miss C. E. Pilkington, Hon. Secretary)
The Close
Addington Park, Nr Maidstone, Kent ME19 5BL
☎ 0732 843589

The Seekers Trust is a Centre for Prayer and Spiritual Healing founded in 1925. Prayer Circles of 30 minutes' duration are held throughout the day, and those on the Trust's lists tune in at the same time, wherever they may be. Contact healing is available by appointment. Monthly lectures and bi-annual conferences are held, and the Trust also runs a ten-week healing course.

Publication: 'Beyond', three times annually.

THE SUFI HEALING ORDER

(Carol Simco)
102 Kingsway
Petts Wood, Nr Orpington, Kent
☎ 0689 20644

The Order aims to spread the practice of healing through the Holy Spirit. The message of the Order's founder Hazrat Inayat Khan is to teach man to discover the divinity that is in him. The Order performs the healing service, and shares practices of purification, light, sound and attunement to the masters. There is a weekly healing service in each centre. Regular seminars are held in London. The two main centres are at 10 Beauchamp Avenue, Leamington Spa and 58 St Stephens Gardens, London, W2. The head of the Sufi Healing Order in England, Sarida Brown, is available to lecture.

Publication: 'The Flute', from Joyce Purcell, The Sufi Order in the West, Barton Farm, Bradford-on-Avon.

THAMES VALLEY NATURAL HEALTH CENTRE

c/o 20 Shottesbrooke
Waltham Road
White Waltham, Berks
☎ 062882 4329

The Centre's aim is to help people realize their potential and responsibility towards their own health and well-being. Lectures, courses, seminars, workshops related to natural health, personal growth and responsibility are open to the public.

Publication: Quarterly newsletter.

TOTNES NATURAL HEALTH CENTRE

69 Fore Street
Totnes, Devon, TQ9 5EA
☎ 0803 864587

The Centre offers specialized services in reflexology, counselling, healing, massage and diet and can provide speakers and workshop leaders. Classes are held at the Centre and the group provides an index on other related organizations.

TOUCH FOR HEALTH

(Brian H. Butler)
39 Browns Road
Surbiton, Surrey KT5 8ST
☎ 01 399 3215

Classes in practical preventive holistic health care are open to the public, as is individual health care. Specialized services are natural preventive and crisis health care, musculo-skeletal and allergy-dietary. Information is also available on applied kinesiology. Small groups might be able to meet at the above address; Mr Butler is available for lectures and workshops. Training programmes are run for individuals, along with weekend and week-long residential courses.

THE TRADITIONAL ACUPUNCTURE CLINIC

188 Old Street
London EC1
☎ 01 251 4429

The clinic which operates from London's East-West Centre provides a treatment service based upon traditional Chinese methods and can also provide an information service on its subject area.

THE VEGETARIAN SOCIETY(UK) LTD

53 Marloes Road
London, W8 6LA
☎ 01 937 7739

The Society is an educational organization and registered charity providing information on all aspects of vegetarianism. Cookery courses, lectures and social events are open to the public. The Society runs a bookshop and has speakers willing to give talks to local groups. It can also provide researchers with names and addresses of organizations concerned with food, health, farming and animal welfare.

Publications: 'The Vegetarian', the journal of the Society; Leaflets, cookbooks; 'International Vegetarian Handbook', a directory of shops, restaurants, hotels, foods and cosmetics.

THE WELLBEING CENTRE

(Redruth Natural Health Centre)
The Old School House
Churchtown Illogan, Redruth, Cornwall
☎ 0209 842999

The Wellbeing Centre was initiated in 1978 by a group of 12 people, who formed the Self Heal Trust to explore and promote life enhancing alternatives in education, health, nutrition, energy and relationships. They now run courses in massage, acupressure and reflexology and can put enquirers in touch with local natural therapists.

Publication: An informal monthly newsletter and programme.

THE WEST LONDON NATURAL HEALTH CENTRE
4 Highland Avenue
Hanwell, London, W7
☏ 01 575 5723

The WLNHC is part of about 20 similar Centres which exist throughout the country. Each one aims to inform members of the public of the many different therapies which are available, and to encourage doctors, practitioners of natural therapies, lay people, and all who are concerned with medicine to work harmoniously towards an understanding of how to avoid ill-health, and of how actively to promote a state of *good*-health and well-being. Information is accordingly offered on alternative therapies and therapists via lectures, meetings and workshops open to the public.

Publications: Leaflets (10p) on 13 different therapies.

WHITCHURCH CENTRE FOR NATURAL HEALTH
4 Whitchurch Lane
Edgware, Middx, HA8 6JZ
☏ 01 952 9566

The Centre is a health food shop (and stockists of herbal, homeopathic and anthroposophical medicines); a homeopathic dispensary; and a natural health clinic, offering acupuncture, osteopathy, radionics and homeopathy. Qualified practitioners will also provide information on many aspects of health care, diet and healing.

NORTH AMERICA

ALIVE POLARITY PROGRAMS
1880 Lincoln Avenue
Calistoga, California 94515
☏ 707 942 4636

Alive Polarity Programs offers: residential health-building programmes using Alive Polarity to improve physical and emotional fitness; vegetarian resorts including lodging, restaurants and health classes and services; four-day seminars, locally sponsored workshops worldwide; health stores offering a special selection of natural health products, including mail order service. There are several training programmes, the chief of which runs for 6 weeks; and films and cassette tapes describing Alive Polarity and programmes.

Publications: 'Alive Polarity: Healing Yourself and Your Family', Jefferson Campbell; newsletter; 'Alive Polarity', 24-page booklet.

ASSOCIATION FOR HOLISTIC HEALTH
PO Box 9532
San Diego, California 92109
☎ 619 275 2694

The Association is a non-profit California state corporation dedicated to the ideal and goal of seeing holistic health available to all persons. They are dedicated to building a strong professional bridge to the current allopathic medical community until all true healing becomes a 'oneness' – instead of symptom amelioration only. They believe that people are responsible for their own healing in relationship with the practitioner. The Association is a volunteer membership organization receiving no outside funding, acting as an information agency and running workshops open to the public.

Publications: Newsletter, 'Focus'; National Directory of Holistic Health Practitioners.

BIOFEEDBACK INSTITUTE OF L.A.
(Marjorie K. Toomin PhD)
6399 Wilshire Blvd # 900
Los Angeles, California 90048
☎ 213 933 9451

The Institute offers biofeedback therapy for stress disorders; general psycho-therapy and family counselling; professional training, seminars and classes for people who wish to add biofeedback therapy to their professional skills, and some information on other biofeedback facilities. Marjorie Toomin and Sandra Thomson, Ed.D. are available to speak at outside functions.

HAWAII HEALTH NET
(c/o Nancy Strode)
1487 Hiikala Place, # 17
Honolulu, Hawaii 96816
☎ 808 735 3929

The Hawaii Health Net is an open communications network of persons whose purpose is the sharing of information about health and the future. They identify with a growing number who search for alternatives to the present health care system – alternatives which reflect a desire and increasing ability to control one's own destiny, to be responsible for one's own life. It is believed that the present disease-oriented, professionalism-dominated medical model is being transformed into one which *promotes health* – i.e. individual and social well-being. The Hawaii Health Net will refer those seeking alternative healthing methods (self-help) to resources known to them.

HERITAGE STORE
317 Laskin Road
Virginia Beach, Virginia 23451
☎ 804 428 0100

Although the Heritage Store maintains a retail facility which offers a wide variety of health foods, herbs and related items for general sale, their primary function is to act as a manufacturer and distributor for the various unique compounds and rare proprietary medications recommended in the trance readings of Edgar Cayce. The shop will ship world wide, on an individual basis, as well as to retail stores and to health food distributor outlets. The Heritage Store has lists of stores and doctors who buy Cayce products from them, and of working psychics.

HIPPOCRATES WORLD HEALTH INSTITUTE
25 Exeter Street
Boston, Massachusetts 02116
☎ 617 267 9525

Founded by Dr Ann Wigmore, DD, ND, HWHO is an educational, humanitarian, non-profit organization devoted to the physical, mental and spiritual development of mankind through a living uncooked diet. Students come from every continent to learn about sprouting, fermenting, composting and living enzyme food, and return home to teach others.

HOMEOPATHIC EDUCATIONAL SERVICES

2124 Kittredge Street
Berkeley, California 94704
☎ 415 845 2206

HES have published six books on homeopathic medicine, and distribute at least 40 others and numerous cassette tapes. They specialize in offering only the best books in the field, by mail order, for health professionals and consumers; they can also provide information of other homeopathic organizations and schools. Workshops are occasionally offered, and HES also co-sponsor conferences. Dana Ullman, MPH (Masters in Public Health, UC Berkeley) has taught homeopathy since 1975 and will speak at outside functions.

FRIENDLY HILLS FELLOWSHIP (MEADOWLARK)

26126 Fairview Avenue
Hemet, California 92343
☎ 7214 927 1343

Meadowlark's primary objective is the rediscovery of the Whole Person. An individual's health is regarded as a balance of well-being in body, mind and spirit. A combination of medicine, psychology, spirituality and the arts provides the means for attaining a higher level of wellness.

The Meadowlark programme, for live-in guests, specializes in meditation, group dynamics, yoga and other body-awareness exercises, nutritional and psychological counselling. Special classes are held, as are occasional workshops and lecture series at the Holistic Health Center. Evarts Loomis, MD and James Kwako, MD are available for lectures, and there is a film, 'Healing the Whole Person'.

Publications: Quarterly newsletter; 'Healing for Everyone', Evarts G. Loomis.

INTERNATIONAL HOLISTIC CENTER, INC./ARIZONA NETWORKING NEWS

PO Box 15103
Phoenix, Arizona 85060
☎ 602 957 3322

International Holistic Center, Inc. and Arizona Networking News offers Holistic networking information through its publications 'Holistic HELP Handbook' and the 'Arizona Networking News', published quarterly. The Center also has 90-minute cassette tapes (e.g. Polarity Energy Balancing Exercises, What is Holistic Health?, Indoor Gardening for Survival). The IHC founder, Stanley Steven Kalson, travels worldwide to connect people and ideas for greater harmony. The modalities used for channelling this message of the New Age are through body, mind and spirit, 'learn by doing' experiences. The Center offers workshops, lectures and seminars worldwide based upon the holistic principles outlined in the 'Holistic HELP Handbook'. Some of these principles include indoor and outdoor gardening for survival, low-cost vegetarian health recipes, polarity and energy flow techniques, and world networking resources. For a teacher in your area, contact IHC. Monthly networking meetings are helping people connect in Phoenix, Arizona. Training programmes are run based on the concepts of body, mind and spirit integration through holistic practices. There is a slide show on networking and holistic living, a 21-minute film, 'Health Through Living Foods', and a Speaker's Bureau for all subjects relating to New Age business, health and metaphysics.

KRIPALU CENTER FOR HOLISTIC HEALTH/ KRIPALU YOGA RETREAT
(Yogi Amrit Desai, founder-director)
PO Box 120
Summit Station, Pennsylvania 17979
☎ 717 754 3051/717 754 3611

This is a residential holistic health and yoga community offering year-round educational and specialized training programmes to the public as well as professional health services. Specialized services are offered in holistic health care, massage, polarity therapy, homeopathy, yoga therapy, all of which are open to the public.
   Three training programmes are run: for yoga teachers (at three levels), bodywork certification training, and counselling certification training. Extensive outside workshops are available on all aspects of holistic health and yoga; seminars are also conducted by the founder-director throughout the world on request.

Publications: 'Kripalu Yoga Quest' (newspaper); 'Self Health Guide'; 'Kripalu Kitchen Cookbook', and others.

LEARNING FOR HEALTH
(Dennis T. Jaffe, PhD)
1314 Westwood Boulevard, Suite 107
Los Angeles, California 90024
☎ 213 474 6929

Learning for Health is a psychosomatic medicine clinic providing psychological services for people with physical illness and stress-related difficulties. Modalities include family therapy, relaxation training, hypnosis, guided imagery, biofeedback, stress management and health education/ self-care workshops. Specialized services are offered in stress management, and marriage and family therapy to individuals, couples, families, and group psychotherapy. Dr Jaffe is available to talk on stress management in organizations, etc.

THE LIGHTED WAY

1515 Palisades Drive, Suite N
Pacific Palisades, California, 90272
☎ 213 459 5861

The Lighted Way is an Ashram, a School for Discipleship Training, working with the Radiation of The Divine Mother and The Hierarchy. Services include Tarot readings, astrology, numerology and touch for health.

Publications: 'The Lighted Way Messenger'; 'Testament of the Light'.

MU-NE-DOWK FOUNDATION, INC.

13111 Lax Chapel Road
Kiel, WI 53042
☎ 414 894 2339

The Foundation is an ecumenical, non-political organization. It rents facilities to those with a spiritual orientation or educational purpose, and can provide teachers qualified in healing, foods and nutrition.

Publication: 'Crystal Light'.

PASADENA AWARENESS CENTER

Office: 1083 Atchison Street
Pasadena, California 91104
Public Meetings: Lounge of Methodist Church, 500 East Colorado
Pasadena, California

The Pasadena Awareness Center is a New Age activity devoted to the proposition that man is an integrated physical, emotional, mental and spiritual whole being – not a collection of segments and parts. While recognizing man's acute immediate needs and problems, and providing help and assistance to cope with them, the group's ultimate goal is prevention of these difficulties through encouragement of the individual's acceptance of responsibility for his own health, emotional maturity and spiritual awareness.

The Center presents public meetings every Wednesday evening at 8.00 p.m. Featured each week are people who are innovators in the exciting developments transpiring in spiritual psychic healing, cosmic energies, parapsychology, metaphysics, esoteric studies and spiritual unfoldment pertinent to the holistic concept. These lectures are followed by healing sessions conducted by staff members and guest psychics and healers.

The scope of services comprising the complete programme includes research and study, reference and information, referrals, training, teaching, classes, group work and private sessions in such fields as health, natural healing, constructive thinking, exercise, manipulative therapies, nutrition and counseling.

Publication: Pasadena Awareness Center monthly bulletin.

SHIATSU EDUCATION CENTER OF AMERICA
52 W 55 Street
New York City, NY 10019
☎ 212 582 3424

The Centre teaches Oha Shiatsu to the public. A two-year training programme is available.

Publications: 'Do It Yourself Shiatsu'; 'Zen Shiatsu'.

SOLANA CENTER FOR TOTAL HEALTH
312 South Cedros
Solana Beach, California 92075
☎ 714 755 6681

The Solana Center for Total Health is a complete health care clinic which specializes in combining traditional medicine with advanced healing approaches. The staff is comprised of medical doctors, chiropractors, emotional therapists, an optometrist, registered nurses, nutritionists, physical therapists, and other health professionals.

UNIVERSAL DIVINE CENTER
Camp Cody's Adult Health & Fitness Center
West Ossipee, New Hampshire 03890
☎ 603 539 4997

There is certified instruction in yoga, physical fitness and nutrition, all open to the general public. The Center is a total resort, with modern health spa facilities. Speakers are available for functions outside the Center to talk on spiritual healing and meditation.

EUROPE

EAST-WEST CENTRE
Achtergracht 17
Amsterdam, Holland
☎ 24 02 03

The Centre holds classes in Eastern healing techniques. Attention is focused on acupressure, massage and diagnosis. Macrobiotic cooking is a central feature to the East-West Centre as are the teachings of Michio Kushi and the techniques of shiatsu. A macro store can be found on the premises.

3HO GURU RAM DAS ASHRAM
C/O Guru Meher Singh Khalsa
Via Degli Spagnoli 24
R-00186
Rome, Italy
☎ 656 5805

Runs classes in acupuncture, astrology, homeopathy, martial arts, massage, meditational music, nutrition and yoga. Classes of kundalini yoga as given by Yogi Bhajan are integrated into the Centre's schedule.

WILHELM REICH CENTRE
Viale Milizie 38
00132 Rome, Italy
☎ 06 3563448

A teaching Centre based around the ideas of Wilhelm Reich offering courses throughout the year which include bioenergetics, encounter, dance and meditation. The Centre can provide information on body therapy, holistic philosophy and character analysis.

REST OF THE WORLD

ALTERNATIVE MEDICAL CENTRE
195 Bourke Street
Darlinghurst
New South Wales, Australia
☎ 335453

This particular centre offers treatments/services and also acts in a consultative capacity in the following areas: herbal and homeopathic remedies, naturopathy and osteopathy. The centre also facilitates encounter groups.

Publication: Regular programme of activities and therapies.

DOUBLE BAY HEALTH CENTRE
17 Know Street
Double Bay
☎ 363579 New South Wales, Australia

The centre (also a college) has a wide range of treatments within the healing spectrum. These include acupuncture, hydrotherapy, iridology, massage, nutrition and zone therapy. Training as well as consultation is offered in these wide-ranging areas.

COSMIC EDUCATION CENTRE
23 Collins Street
Surrey Hills
2010 New South Wales, Australia
☎ 2122152

This organization specializes in the fields of esoteric healing, I Ching, meditation, philosophy, Tarot and yoga. Regular programmes and courses are held.

ESSENCE OF HEALTH
Box 180
Westville, 3630
South Africa
☎ 011 727221

The purpose of this group is to research and disseminate the truth regarding man's natural food, so that he can achieve his full potential. Specialized services are offered in yoga and nature cure. They also distribute 800 books and can provide films on yoga.

YOGA CLINIC
53 Collins Street
Tasmania 7001
Australia

The clinic offers therapy based upon yoga practices and incorporates these into its pre-natal and post-natal classes.

2

GROWTH AND HUMAN POTENTIAL

INTRODUCTION
BY SABINE KURJO

When a seed becomes a flower, there is no question what kind of flower it will become. Likewise, a young rabbit or an elephant will grow into who they are meant to become without any doubt. One wonders therefore, why human beings don't *naturally* become who they are meant to be, why they do not naturally develop all their potential, all their best qualities.

Abraham Maslow was among those psychologists who set out to study happy, healthy, creative and productive people in the late 1950s in California, which gave rise to publications on what was termed 'humanistic psychology' or the 'human potential movement'. In fact, Maslow defined a hierarchy of needs which he suggests has to be satisfied in every human being living a full and satisfactory life. Once basic needs for food and shelter are satisfied, a sense of community, acceptance and respect needs fulfillment, and beyond those psychological needs comes the need for self-actualization and self-realization. C. G. Jung calls this need 'individuation' – a process which takes time and courage, and requires looking at oneself, facing one's shadow, one's 'negative' sides, feelings and sub-personalities as well as all suppressed pain.

However, the rewards are worth it. The characteristics of self-actualized people are a more efficient perception of reality and more comfortable relations with it; acceptance of self, others and nature; spontaneity, problem centering, detachment, independence of culture and environment, continued freshness of appreciation, limitless horizons, deep but selective social relationships, social feeling, democratic character structure, ethical certainty, a non-hostile sense of humour and creativeness.

To develop one's human potential, to make a work of art of one's life – this is what growth centres propose, offering a wide range of techniques and methods. They all aim at improving one's relationship with oneself, others and the universe. Thus, the terms – intrapersonal, interpersonal and transpersonal relationships are used, to highlight these dimensions of man which all need attention and care.

In general, school education does not provide for ways of developing authenticity, creativity and self-responsibility. And after school, adult education does not offer too much for the whole living person in the process of becoming either. It is therefore fortunate that psychological methods developed in the West merge with spiritual traditions of the Orient in the spectrum of techniques to be practised in order to follow one's innate need for self-realization.

A shift of values and paradigms is occurring during the process of personal transformation towards maturity and self-realization. This shift has been described in depth by Marilyn Ferguson in her book 'The Aquarian Conspiracy – Personal and Social Transformation in the 1980's'. The new consciousness shows, for example, in the shift from emphasis on efficiency and the production of goods to an emphasis on human values; from the body and mind as being separate to an holistic bodymind perspective where the mind is a co-equal factor to wellness and illness, from seeing the body as a machine to perceiving the bodymind as a dynamic system – an energy field within energy fields; from considering the healing professional as an emotionally neutral authority figure to seeing the professional as a caring, sympathetically involved partner in the healing process; from primary trust in quantifiable data and rational cognitive thinking to the additional values of subjective, intuitive, qualitative, metaphoric and holistic ways of knowing; from learning as social necessity for a specified time in order to acquire minimal skills, to training for a particular role – a 'product' orientation – to learning as a lifelong process, only partly related to schools – a continuous journey; from primary concern with the norm, with competition, with 'I win – you lose' to interest in individual self-actualization, limit-testing, co-operation, a 'win-win' mentality; from manipulation and domination over nature to co-operation, awareness and respect for our environment.

This shift of perspective is based on the shift of experiencing trust rather than fear. Trusting oneself, others and the universe rather than being afraid results in changes of attitude with far-reaching effects in society: peace instead of war, communication rather than separation, sharing the resources of the planet in a global society rather than exploiting for nationalistic purposes.

The personal and spiritual growth of a person can be described as the transformation from a dependent human being to one who knows and feels that he/she is in charge of his/her life and acts upon it. I have experienced this change myself after a four-year Jungian analysis and a car accident which prevented me from pursuing my career as a computer programmer. I took workshops in humanistic psychology wherever possible and got so much out of it for myself, that I wanted to pass this opportunity on to the world. I thus created the growth centre 'Vision Humaniste' in Geneva, and the 'European Association for Humanistic Psychology' grew out of the enthusiasm generated at the European Conferences on Humanistic Psychology which I organized in Geneva. I am now setting up the Peace Network for everybody interested in peace and a more humane world.

UK

THE ARTHUR FINDLAY COLLEGE
Stansted Hall
Stanstead, Essex CM24 8UB
☎ 0279 813636

A residential college for psychic study, owned by the Spiritualist National Union. Courses range from physical phenomena and mediumship to healing and meditation. The college also trains mediums and speakers. Situated in a large stately home, its facilities are available to other groups.

THE ASSOCIATION FOR HUMANISTIC PSYCHOLOGY
5 Layton Road
London N1
☎ 01 226 4240

The Association has a membership of both lay and professional people involved in promoting the ideas of humanistic psychology in Britain. There are affiliated associations all over the world and activities include an ongoing programme of events and programmes. These cover such fields as Gestalt, meditation, bioenergetics, primal integration and aspects of bodywork.

Publications: A regular programme of events and news.

ASTROLOGICAL ASSOCIATION
(Research Section)
36 Tweedy Road
Bromley, Kent BR1 3PP
☎ 01 464 3853

The Association encourages astrological research and astrological application. It helps professionals do their jobs better and ensures that high standards are maintained. Information on all aspects of astrology is available.

Publications: 'The Astrological Journal'; 'Transit'; 'Correlation'.

THE ASTROLOGICAL SOCIETY
c/o 66 Albert Road
Levenshulme, Manchester 19
☎ 061 225 4621

Concerned with basic astrological interpretation and advanced techniques including esoteric and galactic astrology. Study groups are held in several cities.

BARTON FARM
Sufi House
Bradford-on-Avon, Wilts
☎ 022 16 5281

The Centre studies the Sufi Path through meditation, healing, universal worship, dancing and pottery. Small courses are arranged and healing and individual guidance is available.

Publication: 'The Flute' newsletter.

BEANSTALK
c/o 128 Byres Road
Hillhead, Glasgow
☎ 041 334 5846

Beanstalk operates as a collective offering weekend workshops, evening courses and individual sessions in massage, Reichian therapy, postural integration and hypnosis.

Publication: 'Beanstalk' – newsletter.

CENTRE FOR ALTERNATIVE EDUCATION AND RESEARCH
Rosemerryn, Lamorna
Penzance, Cornwall
☎ 073672 530

CAER is a self-sufficient growth centre in magical Cornish countryside, providing the highest quality groups and attracting leading figures in the human potential movement. Workshops are mainly residential and are run in a friendly, country-house atmosphere. Services are available in personal growth, yoga, transpersonal psychology, relationships and human potential research. Training programmes are also available for yoga teachers and astrologers.

Publication: Courses and workshops programme published three times a year.

CENTRE FOR CONSCIOUS LIVING

4 The Causeway
Chippenham, Wilts, SN15 3BT
☎ 0249 50789

The Centre is for people who are seeking a more aware state of consciousness and a more meaningful way of living, through meditation, yoga, right diet, the study of human communication and other practices that encourage the evolution of mankind. Week and weekend courses are available and a health food shop is run from the Centre.

CHURCHILL CENTRE

22 Montagu Street
London W1U 1TB
☎ 01 402 9475

Provides training courses in massage, relaxation, foot reflex therapy and aromatherapy. Appointments can be made for physical and psychological treatments. Offers certificate courses in health care and related areas.

Publication Newsletter available to students.

THE COLLEGE OF PSYCHIC STUDIES

16 Queensberry Place
London SW7 2EB
☎ 01 589 3292/3203

The College is a source of reliable information and guidance on psychic and paranormal matters and healing. It endeavours to work for better understanding of them, and to help members to develop and enrich the inner side of their natures, so making their life more meaningful.

Publications: Journal, 'Light'.

CONTEXT RESEARCH

BM/Searchers
London WC1N 3XX

Context investigates the implications of reincarnation and other planes of existence for psychology and therapy. It collects and distributes relevant information to enquirers and also welcomes information for the Summary it will be publishing in 1983. Three booklets are currently available, 60p each. It holds discussion groups in Birmingham, including group dynamics workshops. Context also offers free counselling by post (s.a.e. appreciated).

FOUNDATION OF THE CHURCH OF RELIGIOUS SCIENCE
20 Cassel Avenue
Poole, Dorset BH13 6JD
☎ 0202 764431

The mission of this church is to make God real in life and re-establish the greatness within the British people by improving the quality of life through the demonstration of faith, harmony, prayer, abundance and love. Spiritual healing and counselling is available as is guidance and aid in establishing affiliate study groups. The church holds training courses in science of mind and healing, and runs workshops on prosperity relationships.

Publication: 'The Olive Branch', newsletter.

GALE CENTRE FOR CREATIVE THERAPY
Whitakers Way
Loughton, Essex
☎ 01 508 9344

The Centre offers personal psychotherapy using creative therapy. It provides lessons and workshops in the Wolfshon method of voice production and therapy. Training courses are available for members of the caring professions in all aspects of the creative therapies, especially psychodrama and art therapy.

GERDA BOYESEN CENTRE FOR BIODYNAMIC PSYCHOLOGY AND PSYCHOTHERAPY
Acacia House
Centre Avenue, The Vale
London W3
☎ 01 743 2437

The Centre provides group and individual therapy, a massage clinic, a training school preparing students for the diploma in biodynamic psychology. An open programme of events is run throughout the year.

Publication: 'Journal of Biodynamic Psychology'.

INNER LIGHT CONSCIOUSNESS IN EUROPE
Moorhurst
South Holmwood
Dorking, Surrey RH5 4LJ
☎ 0306 6663

ILC teaches the techniques evolved by Paul Solomon for getting in touch with the creative intelligence which is a part of each one of us. These are based on a dynamic which enables one to shed unwanted habits and beliefs and become a cause rather than an effect and create one's own experience. Full training programmes are available.

Publications: 'Supportive Lifestyles News'.

INSTITUTE OF PSYCHOSYNTHESIS
Nan Clarks Lane
Mill Hill
London NW7
☎ 01 959 3372

The Institute was founded to provide in-depth experience in the principles and practice of psychosynthesis, for individuals concerned with their own growth and practising professionals from fields such as medicine, psychology, education, religion and business.

Psychosynthesis views each person as a whole, seeing both personal and spiritual aspects as important. It recognizes that in each of us is a transpersonal essence or Self and its purpose is to manifest this essence as fully as possible in the world of everyday living.

The Institute runs many courses and classes and offers professional training and counselling.

Publications: These include programmes of activities and also books on Psychosynthesis by Dr Roberto Assagioli and others.

THE LOTHLORIEN TRUST
Corsock, Castle Douglas
Kirkcudbrightshire, Scotland DG7 3DR
☎ 064 44 644

This is a small family-based community operating around a rural way of life with a basically Christian background. People are invited to learn and grow with them. There are no formal training courses.

Publication: A newsletter is published once a year.

MAYO SCHOOL OF ASTROLOGY
Ridge Cottage
8 Stoggy Lane
Plympton, Devon

The School provides astrological correspondence courses to students all over the world. Its aim is to produce students who can apply their knowledge in modern scientific and psychological terms.

MEDINA RAJNEESH
Herringswell
Bury St Edmunds, Suffolk IP28 6SW
☎ 0638 750234

KALPTARU RAJNEESH THERAPY CENTRE
28 Oak Village
London NW5 4QN
☎ 01 267 8304, 485 3216, 485 4206

Medina Rajneesh is an educational facility created by the British disciples of Bhagwan Shree Rajneesh. It is a holistic centre offering methods for work on the self ranging from hypno-regression to acupuncture, Vipassana meditation to Neo-Reichian techniques. Medina functions as a community, and is set in the Suffolk countryside.

Kalptaru Rajneesh Therapy Centre is the London centre for the work of Bhagwan Shree Rajneesh. Its function is to make available facilities for Bhagwan's meditations and group techniques and to give access to his words through taped discourses and books.

MEHER BABA ASSOCIATION
The Boathouse, Ranelagh Drive
Twickenham, Middx
☎ 01 892 1118

The Association is a non-sectarian body devoted to Avatar Meher Baba and is pledged to extend, develop, expand and put into practice the spiritual guidance given and humanitarian work carried out by him during his lifetime.

Regular meetings are held and books and tapes are available.

MIND DEVELOPMENT ASSOCIATION
5 Haig Lane, Mandercey Court
Church Crookham, Hants
☎ 02514 28106

This is an association of experienced biofeedback researchers, qualified therapists and teachers of various systems of mental development and personal growth. The group is dedicated to the unfoldment of human potential through the conscious integration of body, mind and spirit. Comprehensive courses are available for dynamic growth and greater awareness.

THE OPEN CENTRE

188 Old Street
London EC1
☎ 01 278 6783 ex 3

This is a well-established growth centre unique in that it provides a variety of different therapy and movement groups within the broad spectrum of humanistic psychology. The Open Centre operates as a collective of group leaders, sharing administrative work as well as skills in working with people. There are eight full-time leaders and two associates. Services are available in encounter, bioenergetics, massage, dance, transactional analysis, Gestalt, primal integration, tai-do and tai-chi.

Courses and training programmes are provided in these areas.

Publication: 'The Open Centre Handbook'.

PSYCHOSYNTHESIS AND EDUCATION TRUST

50 Guildford Road
London SW8 2BU
☎ 01 720 7800

The Trust was founded under the guidance of Dr Roberto Assagioli in 1965. Its objectives are to make psychosynthesis available to the public through educational, scientific and charitable means. The Trust disseminates information on psychosynthesis and investigates the use of higher psychological functions such as intuition, inspiration, mental and artistic creativity. There are courses throughout the year and individual counselling services.

REBIRTH SOCIETY

c/o 143 Willifield Way
London NW11 6XY
☎ 01 455 4063

Rebirthing is a simple, yet dramatically powerful, technique for personal growth. It is a breathing technique which enables you to let go of long-held tensions quickly and easily, and to allow more love, joy and pleasure into your life. The Rebirth Society provides information and ensures high professional standards amongst practitioners of rebirthing.

SAROS – FOUNDATION FOR INTERPRETATION OF KNOWLEDGE

Hardwick Hall
Hardwick Square South
Buxton, Derbyshire

The Foundation holds weekend residential courses covering such areas as Kabbalah, astrology, meditation, spindizzy dancing and palmistry. There are study groups in Manchester, London, Cambridge, Oxford and Bristol.

Publication: Saros prospectus.

THE SEMPERVIVUM TRUST

c/o The Salisbury Centre
2 Salisbury Place
Edinburgh 8, Scotland
☎ 031 667 5438

The Trust is a network of people of all ages based mostly in Scotland, committed to psychological and spiritual understanding and growth. It organizes annual autumn, Lenten and Easter schools which are open to all. Activities include dream groups, meditation, group work, art and dance.

Publication: Sempervivum magazine.

SILVA MIND CONTROL LTD

BCM Meditation
London WC1N 3XX
☎ 01 493 1815

The Silva Mind Control method uses dynamic meditation to control the mind and develop its unlimited powers for better health, happiness, success etc. Silva Mind control seeks to provide positive solutions to all our problems. There are currently over 3,500,000 graduates all over the world and in London 5 courses a year are held.

SOCIETY FOR PSYCHICAL RESEARCH

1 Adam & Eve Mews
Kensington
London W8
☎ 01 937 8984

The first of the psychic research groups, which investigates and reports on all forms of psychic phenomena. The society has researched poltergeists, hauntings, mind over matter, mediumship and much more.

Publication: Journal.

THE SOLAR QUEST

Cove
Tiverton, Devon
☎ 0398 31223

A registered charity offering a highway to those seeking peace of mind. Various healing services are offered as well as counselling and advice to members. Membership is worldwide and correspondence courses are available.

Publications: Several introductory booklets.

THE TEILHARD CENTRE

81 Cromwell Road
London SW7 5BW
☎ 01 370 6660

The Teilhard Centre is a non-profitmaking organization established for the critical study, dissemination and development of the evolutionary thought of Pierre Teilhard de Chardin, and its application to contemporary human problems and the shaping of the future. The Centre puts on lectures, courses and conferences.

Publication: 'The Teilhard Review'.

THE TRANSPERSONAL PSYCHOLOGY CENTRE

The Studio
8 Elsworthy Terrace
London, NW3

The centre runs a series of specialized workshops covering a range of subjects including myths, chakras, meditation and archetypes. To participate in its workshops it is necessary to have previous experience in one or two of its basic programmes.

THE VEGAN SOCIETY LTD

9 Mawddwy Cottages
Minllyn Dinas Mawddwy
Machynlleth, Wales SY20 9LW
☎ 06504 255

The Society promotes a way of living on the products of the plant kingdom direct, so that animals may be freed from cruel exploitation and the earth's resources used economically to give both a healthy sustainable diet and a more aware compassionate lifestyle in the service of life. The Vegans run cookery courses and put on lectures and film shows.

Publication: 'The Vegan', quarterly magazine, and several books on the Vegan way.

NORTH AMERICA

ANDERSON RESEARCH FOUNDATION INC.
2942 Francis Avenue
Los Angeles, California 90005
☎ 213 387 9164

The Anderson Research Foundation, as a non-profit corporation, is dedicated to research in the non-limited, multiple approach to life enhancement. It sponsors the Precision Psychodrama Institute and the Anderson Research Center (ARC). It evaluates all methods of life enhancement as to efficiency, cost in time and funds, effort, threat, acceptability, etc., using General Semantics and other systems. The Foundation also explores the use of isolation tanks for in-depth experiences.

Publication: Bi-monthly newsletter.

ASSOCIATION FOR DEVELOPMENT OF HUMAN POTENTIAL
Box 60
Porthill, Idaho 83853
☎ 604 227 9224

Affiliated with
YASODHARA ASHRAM SOCIETY
Box 9
Kootenay Bay, British Columbia, Canada VOB 1XO

The main objective is to investigate the nature of human consciousness and the interrelationship of the physical, mental-emotional and spiritual aspects of the human being. Yoga study and teacher training are offered, as well as group growth workshops and community residency.

THE ASSOCIATION FOR TRANSPERSONAL PSYCHOLOGY

PO Box 3049
Stanford, California 94305
☎ 415 327 2066

The Association for Transpersonal Psychology is a group of individuals who share an interest in transpersonal psychology and transpersonal values. Some members are interested in, or are practising professionally, in psychology, education, research and spiritual disciplines. Others are philosophers or friends who support the transpersonal orientation. The Association provides a vehicle for those who want to communicate with each other about their transpersonal ideas, experiences, work and process.

An annual conference is held each summer, to provide an opportunity for members to meet with colleagues and friends and to learn about transpersonal activities throughout the USA and abroad. Over fifty different presentations, workshops and seminars are presented during the weekend event. Special one-day institutes are held before the conference.

Publication: 'Journal of Transpersonal Psychology'.

CENTRE FOR INTEGRATIVE PSYCHOLOGY

215 Beach Street, # 307
Santa Cruz, California 95060

The Centre offers personal and spiritual growth counselling and works with PhD students specializing in transpersonal psychology and psychological counselling, taking a universal context into consideration.

CHURCH OF WORLD MESSIANITY

9605 Kenmore Avenue
Los Angeles, California 90006
☎ 213 382 2173

The objective of World Messianity is to help humanity pass through the present chaotic transitional period taking us from an Age of Darkness into a new Daylight Age. It is the Church's desire to work co-operatively with all like-minded groups and individuals in eliminating disease, poverty and conflict and to construct an ideal world which they believe is part of a divine plan for this planet. The Church's membership stands at 800,000.

Publication: Newsletter.

CONTINUUM FOUNDATION

721 W. Woodbury Road
Altadena, California 91001
☎ 213 794 3433

The Foundation is based around the travelling exhibition, 'Continuum –
The Immortality Principle' in the USA. It distributes films, tapes and the
book of the same name. In the UK, Unilight Productions (57 Warescot
Road, Brentwood, Essex CM15 9HH) distributes the video film of the
exhibition.

THE CORTES CENTRE FOR HUMAN DEVELOPMENT

Box 48295, Bentall Centre
Vancouver, BC, Canada V7X 1A1
☎ 604 224 0715

The Cortes Centre for Human Development is a registered society which
offers public workshops for personal and professional development. The
Cortes Centre provides the environment and skill-training necessary for
individuals to enrich the quality of their lives through self-discovery,
self-responsibility and growth in relationships. The consulting staff is a
network of professionals trained in personal counselling and group dynamics, each of whom has additional training and experience in a specialized field.

DEVALLE INSTITUTE OF GROWTH

(Lady Suzanne DeValle DD)
1024 Highview Avenue
Manhattan Beach, California 90266
☎ 213 545 0063

Suzanne DeValle/DeValle Institute of Growth (founded 1964) offers, in
company or on location, stress management training and student training
seminars. The Institute presents workshops in varied areas every month,
and offers private consultations daily and weekend retreats. Also available are mail order tapes and workbooks for weight, smoking, game or
business improvement, memory, healing, financial success. The programmes are designed for individuals, organizations, corporations and
clubs.

ESALEN INSTITUTE

Big Sur, California 93920
☎ 408 667 2335

Esalen is one of the largest growth centres in the world offering programmes in Gestalt practice, holistic health and spiritual emergence. It is a residential community handling several thousand visitors each year.

HARTLEY FILM FOUNDATION INC.
Cat Rock Road
Cos Cob, CI 06807
☎ 203 869 1818

The Foundation produces and distributes New Age films on philosophy, psychology, religion and holistic health. In the UK Unilight Productions (57 Warescot Road, Brentwood, Essex CM15 9HH) acts as distributor.

INSTITUTE FOR CONSCIOUSNESS AND MUSIC TRAINING SEMINARS
7027 Bellona Avenue
Baltimore, Maryland 21212
☎ 301 377 7525

The Institute trains individuals to use in counselling situations a technique called Guided Imagery and Music. GIM helps individuals discover and come to understand the imaginal realm of the unconscious with the help of carefully selected classical music selections. Healing, creativity break-through and spiritual awakening can be assisted by this technique.

Publications: Three monographs by Helen L. Bonny.

INTERNATIONAL ASSOCIATION OF EDUCATORS FOR WORLD PEACE
PO Box 3282, Blue Spring Station
Huntsville, Alabama 35810–0282
☎ 205 539 7205

The Association aims to foster international understanding and world peace, using education as a medium; to further the application of the Universal Declaration of Human Rights through the promotion of several programmes; to broaden international communications at the personal level; and to develop peaceful coexistence.

Publications: 'Peace Progress' (IAEWP Journal of Education); 'Peace Education' (Bulletin); Circulation newsletter.

THE LOVE PROJECT

PO Box 7601
San Diego, California 92107
☎ 714 225 0133

The Project offers learning processes to live and function in universal love. Classes, workshops and intensives are held on a regular basis.

Publication: 'The Seekers' newsletter.

NEW LIFE FOUNDATION

RFD # 2, Box 330
Brooks, Maine 04921

The Foundation holds an annual healing arts festival and runs periodic workshops in specific holistic areas.

Publication: A holistic health paper and directory 'New Life Now'.

NEXUS FOUNDATION

Fairbanks Chapter
PO Box 271
Fairbanks, Alaska 99707
☎ 907 456 4587

The Foundation meets once a month, at members' homes, to have presentations and discussions on esoteric and metaphysical topics of interest to the membership, e.g. dream analysis, regressions. Psychic readings are given on request.

PSYCHOSYNTHESIS TRAINING CENTRE

High Point Foundation
647 North Madison Avenue
Pasadena, California 91101
☎ 213 6811033

The Centre offers a three-year course in Psychosynthesis training, and also runs workshops and seminars. It specializes in holistic psychology, meditation, grief work and preparation for death.

Publication: 'Psychosynthesis in the Classroom'.

SPIRITUAL UNITY MOVEMENT

(subsidiary: Aquarian Age Church of LA)
9575 Canterbury Avenue,
Arleta, California 91331
☎ 213 892 1832

Aquarian Age Church Services (Festivals) offers study and meditation on The Ageless Wisdom. They do not teach dogma, but urge participants to find their own authority within. Discussions are held on reincarnation, cause and effect, rays and initiations, the seven principles of man, etc.

Publication: 'Journey into Light and Joy', by Howard Ray Carey.

EUROPE

APEIRON-INSTITUTET

Drottninggatan 102
S-111 60 Stockholm, Sweden
☎ 08 11 18 99

Running courses in re-creative movement development, Alexander technique, vision improvement (Bates), massage and bodywork. Also longer residential courses, skiing weeks.

ASTROLOGICAL PSYCHOLOGY INSTITUTE

(Bruno and Louise Huber)
Rütistrasse 5
CH-8134 Adliswil, Switzerland
☎ 01 710 37 76

The Institute runs training courses for laymen in astrological psychology, from beginner's level.

Publication: 'Astrolog' magazine for astrological psychology.

CENTRE DE DEVELOPPEMENT DU POTENTIEL HUMAIN

38 Rue de Turenne
75003 Paris, France
☎ 1 277 4331

The Centre can offer specialist services in a number of fields including bio-energetics, Gestalt, primal therapy, rolfing, Reichian work, dance and theatre. Training programmes open to the public in most of these fields.

Publication: 'Training for Reciprocal Work'.

CENTRO STUDI UMANOLOGIA (CSU)
NF Training
Casella Postale 10/200
00144 Rome, Italy
☎ 06 540229

The Centre uses a holistic approach in their work with people and works towards the actualization of one's constructive potential. Courses are offered in primal reintegration, psychoanalysis and psychotherapy.

CREPER
Travesera de Las Corts
188 bajos (B-28)
Barcelona, Spain
☎ 3306067

This is a therapy centre concerned with Gestalt, bioenergetics etc. There is an ongoing programme of workshops, and counselling is available to individuals.

DE KOSMOS
Prins Hendrikkade 142
Amsterdam, The Netherlands
☎ 020 267477

De Kosmos is a centre with about 70,000 visitors per year offering a large variety of courses and programmes to help people deepen and explore their consciousness of body/mind and spirit. Courses include different meditation systems, yoga, tai chi chu'an, aikido, massage, astrology, Zazen, Bach remedies and more. Other programmes include a weekly film, concerts, theatre, poetry and media presentations. Besides these programmes, De Kosmos offers many other facilities: sauna, vegetarian restaurant, natural foodstore, a bookstore, library, art studio and tea-house. The big hall with roofbeams from the eighteenth century looks like a Japanese market place and is the heart of De Kosmos where all the important programmes take place.

Publication: 'Kosmos Nieuwsblad'.

EUROPEAN ASSOCIATION FOR HUMANISTIC PSYCHOLOGY

38 Rue de Turenne
75003 Paris, France
☎ 1 271 8762

The Association promotes the values, philosophy and techniques of humanistic psychology in Europe, as well as holding an annual European conference. It can provide information about techniques, leaders and theory in its field.

GONPO TRANSPERSONAL INSTITUTE

Ohjaajantie 28 C26
Helsinki, Finland
☎ 575 455

The Institute concerns itself with therapeutic schooling and research in connection with spiritual growth. Its work is influenced by both Eastern and Western teachings.

INSTITUTE OF BIOENERGETICS

Via Andrea Doria, 48
Rome, Italy

The Institute propagates the work of Wilhelm Reich through programmes of workshops and lectures concerned with all aspects of Reich's work and related research.

INSTITUTE FOR PLANETARY SYNTHESIS

PO Box 128
CH 1211
Geneva, Switzerland

The Institute is a seed group creating the foundation for people balancing inner spiritual activity and outer objective work for humanity and the planet.

Publication: 'The Path of Planetary Synthesis' – introductory paper.

INSTITUTE OF PSYCHOSYNTHESIS

Via S. Domenico 16
Florence, Italy

The Institute has centres throughout Italy and the world and is concerned with the expression of the transpersonal self or higher Self in everyday life. Workshops, courses, counselling are amongst the activities of the centre which is based on the ideas of its founder – Dr Roberto Assagioli.

SATYAM SHIVAM SUNDARAM
Heinzstraat 23 1
Amsterdam, Holland
☎ 73103

This centre holds workshops on the specialist area of chakric psychology. It also offers courses on meditation, Indian cooking, massage, herbs, sound therapy, etc. A full programme is available.

TRANSFORMATIONS-SEMINARE
Othmarscher Kirchenweg 5
2000 Hamburg 50, West Germany
☎ 040 880 48 30

The Centre is concerned with group and individual therapy and holds weekend workshops on dreams, psychological weight control, past lives and stress management.

Publications: 'Creative Dream Therapy'; 'Weight Control'; 'Stress Management'.

UNITÉ UNIVERSELLE
Center of Ontology and Psychology
22 Rue de Douai
75009 Paris, France
☎ 874 70 89

Dr Mary Sterling founded Unité Universelle in 1946. It is a New Thought Center (ontology and psychology) and publishes a monthly magazine serving all French-speaking countries. Meditation meetings are held weekly.

THE REST OF THE WORLD
AIKIKAI, AIKIDO WORLD HEADQUARTERS
102 Wakamatsu-Cho
Shinjuku-ku
Tokyo 162, Japan
☎ 03 203 9236

World Headquarters of Aikido, also serving as the head office of the

International Aikido Federation, All Japan Aikido Federation, Aikido School, etc. Instruction, seminars and demonstrations of Aikido are offered.

Publications: 'Aikido Shimbun' (in Japanese); 'The Aikido' (in English).

OPEN MIND PUBLICATIONS
c/o Post Office
Glen Forrest, West Australia 6071

The group is involved in writing and publishing books on spiritual matters and also provides counselling services. Its main aim is to promote wholeness on all levels of living.

The Open Mind Group are particularly concerned with research on guided imagery, use of music and developing an education for inner living. Training programmes may be arranged if required.

Publications: 'Cosmic Connection'; 'The Christos Experiment'; 'The Individuation Process'; 'The Legend of the Immortals'.

THE RELAXATION CENTRE
Corner of Brookes and Wickham Streets
Valley
Brisbane
Queensland 4006, Australia

The Centre is concerned with all forms of relaxation and meditation and runs several courses and other regular programmes.

Publication: 'The Centre Within' – newsletter.

RELIGIOUS SCIENCE INTERNATIONAL
PO Box 29014
Sandringham 2131
Johannesburg, South Africa
☎ 640 1313

RSI provides a three-year course in religious science. It holds healing services, inspirational talks and other classes on self-fulfilment.

Publications: Monthly newsletter; 'How to overcome worry' (booklet); 'Speak your word' (positive affirmations).

WORLD UNITY AND SERVICE
PO Box 41338
Craighall 2024, South Africa
☏ 011 48 4988

This organization is concerned with promoting right relationships at all levels and making the universal prayer, 'The Great Invocation', more widely known and used.

3

HOLISTIC EDUCATION

INTRODUCTION
BY GEOFFREY LEYTHAM

Although educational policies and systems may differ, both between and within countries, there still seem to be certain criteria which are fairly universal when curricula and procedures are being considered. One of the most restrictive of these is that the material taught should be amenable to a written examination at the end of the course. If it cannot be examined, then omit it.

This is not unlike the situation in academic and 'scientific' psychology, where measurability is the key criterion for attention. If you cannot measure it, ignore it.

These stresses on measurement and assessment, place undue emphasis on the cognitive aspect of human personality and on verbal fluency, whereas many – if not most – of the really worthwhile aspects of life are concerned with the much less tangible human activities, such as love, aesthetic appreciation and religious experiences. How dull existence would be without these affairs of the heart and intuition. This is not to say that the mental aspect is unimportant, but that to concentrate on it is to give a very biased and boring view of life. This is why education and psychology, as officially presented, are so often dull and uninspiring.

It is not difficult to understand how this state of affairs came about. Education was originally for the privileged few and was a preparation for a professional career. Inertia has led to the perpetuation of the system in spite of vast changes in the number and range of people now eligible for education. Academic psychology, as a newcomer on the university scene, had to prove its scientific respectability, and seems to have got stuck with a model of science that is now quite out of date.

Perhaps one of the main reasons for the continuation of outmoded systems of education and theories of psychology, is that those in control tend to be those that succeed in the system and hence are likely to maintain it. However, if one were to take a detached view of the world today, what sorts of criteria for education would seem most reasonable?

In the Preface to his excellent book, 'Human Teaching for Human Learning: an Introduction to Confluent Education', George Brown says that: 'most people would admit that some educational process is vital (1) for survival and (2) for the enhancement of living.' He refers to the dehumanizing versus humanizing polarity in civilization today and comes down heavily on the side of making education and life more human. 'We see each individual as a unique human being with enormous potential,' he remarks, and asks how can society transmute potentiality into actuality. His answer is that: 'The transmutation process is primarily an educational process.'

In order to understand the requirements of such a transmutation process, it is helpful to have some idea of the stages through which an individual has to pass before achieving the realization of his or her unique potential. One of the most pertinent models in this respect is that put forward by Abraham Maslow – a humanistic psychologist. He suggested that human needs form a hierarchy of prepotency and that 'higher' needs could only take over as 'lower' ones were satisfied or assured of satisfaction. Thus, the physiological needs are most basic, as without air, food and water we would die. The safety needs are the next most urgent, as without shelter and protection it is not easy to survive. Moving upwards from the physical needs to the more emotional ones, our next requirement is for love and a feeling of belonging. The family, and especially the parents, normally provide this, but affectionate relationships are not automatic and many people get stuck at this stage. Maslow next refers to the esteem needs – the more rational appraisal of one's worth as a citizen, and the need to have this worth recognized by others. We can, of course, be a success socially and vocationally without satisfying our own expectations as to what we are capable of achieving.

Maslow called these potent needs the deficiency needs, and regarded their satisfaction as a necessary preliminary to the full emergence of the growth need for self-actualization. Only when an individual feels secure about the general human needs can he or she be free to concentrate on realizing his or her unique potential. Life is a struggle between conformity and uniqueness, with the weighting heavily in favour of the former. Security is demanding but the calls of growth are weak.

This view of the human lot is commensurate with the idea that individuals develop through successive levels of awareness: physical, emotional, mental and intuitive. These correspond well with Jung's four functions of sensation, feeling, thinking and intuition. Although he did not put them in a developmental sequence, Jung did stress that most human problems are due to an imbalance in the development of these functions. For the true Self to emerge, it is necessary to have harmony among the functions, with each having full and conscious use.

What are the implications of all this for education? It is interesting that the word derives from two Latin verbs: 'educare', to bring up, and 'educere', to draw out. The first would seem to apply to the provision of satisfaction for the 'deficiency' needs, while the latter is more concerned with the realization of potential. Perhaps a good motto for education – and it does not only take place in school – would be: 'provide security and encourage growth.'

To achieve successfully the transmutation process that George Brown mentions, those concerned with education should keep in mind the stages through which people develop, and ensure that each individual is treated as a whole person with unique potentiality. Body, feelings, mind and spirit need to be in harmony and balanced for health and wholeness, and only by educating with this in mind can we hope to achieve that enhancement of living that will make survival really worth while.

UK

AQUARIUS TAPES

Carrington Cottage
Bassingham
Lincoln LN5 9JX

Aquarius Tapes is a free lending library of cassette tape recordings of talks and lectures orientated towards the New Age and towards inclusive living.

Publication: Catalogue.

ENGLISH NEW EDUCATION FELLOWSHIP

2 Wilton Grove
New Malden, Surrey KT3 RG6
☎ 01 942 6821

The ENEF is the English section of the World Education Fellowship, a network of progressive educators formed in 1921 to bring about the changes in education that will foster personal development and self-fulfilment of children within the relationships of family, supportive school communities, and a climate of social responsibility and world-awareness.

Publications: The 'New Era' (quarterly educational journal); 'Advances in Understanding the Child'; 'Advances in Understanding the Adolescent'.

THE FRANCIS BACON RESEARCH TRUST

The Dairy Office
Castle Ashby, Northampton, NN7 1LJ
☎ 060 129 331

Conference address:
Stanley Hall
Pebmarsh, Near Halstead
Essex CO9 2LY

The Trust is concerned with making known and actively advancing the Great Instauration – a universal scheme for the gradual and progressive enlightenment of all mankind, put into operation 400 years ago, to lead man into acquiring precise and accurate knowledge about himself, God and nature, both physical and metaphysical, and to promote charity and brotherhood everywhere.

Publications: FBRT Journal; Books/booklets.

KRISHNAMURTI FOUNDATION TRUST LTD
24 Southend Road
Beckenham, Kent BR3 1SD

Arranging talks, meetings and publications of Mr Jiddu Krishnamurti. Meetings take place annually at Brockwood Park Educational Centre, Bramdean, Nr Alresford, Hants.

Publication The works of Krishnamurti.

SALISBURY CENTRE
2 Salisbury Road
Edinburgh EH16 5AB
☎ 031 667 5438

The Salisbury Centre is an open centre where residents live and work together. The Centre runs growth oriented workshops and classes and aims to provide a meditative environment. It also provides accommodation for travellers.

THE SCIENTIFIC AND MEDICAL NETWORK
Lake House
Ockley, Nr Dorking, Surrey RH5 5NS
☎ 0306 711268

An informal international group consisting mainly of scientists and medical doctors, with a seasoning of philosophers, engineers, economists and others. It seeks to extend the framework of contemporary thought beyond ideas at present considered orthodox, aiming at a much more comprehensive, sensitive approach to human problems, including intuitive and spiritual insights. Membership is by invitation.

SOLUNA
Rosewood House
Lydbrook, Forest of Dean, Glos. GL17 9SA
☎ 0594 60595

Soluna provides courses and publications on exploring the inner worlds, healing, spiritual psychology, altered and new states of consciousness and the awareness of a new age. They also offer typesetting and printing/ production services.

Publications: 'Soluna Journal'; 'New Life Directory'.

WORLD GOODWILL

Suite 54, 3 Whitehall Court
London SW1A 2EF
☎ 01 839 4512

World Goodwill has these objectives: to help mobilize the energy of goodwill; to co-operate in the work of preparation for the reappearance of the Christ; to educate public opinion on the causes of the major world problems and to help create the thought-form of solution; to promote the Great Invocation.

Publications: Quarterly newsletter; Commentaries on world problems – (translated into German, Italian, Greek, French, Spanish).

ZANDTHRIF (Psychic and Spiritual Centre)

13 Belgrave Place
Kemp Town, Brighton, BN2 1EL
☎ 0273 694405

This is a centre for psychic and spiritual healing, shiatzu, hypnosis, past lives studies and aura and Tarot reading. Lectures and workshops on these areas are held in South England.

WREKIN TRUST

Dove House
Little Birch, Hereford HR2 8BB
☎ 0981 540224

The Trust arranges courses on the evolution of consciousness, the deeper truths behind the world's great religions, and the Western mystery school tradition. Their workshops encourage the use of hidden knowledge and the development of intuition. The major conferences bridge orthodox materialistic disciplines and the unorthodox spiritual approach to such professional subjects.

Publications: Newsletter; General and specific programmes.

NORTH AMERICA

AQUARIAN RESEARCH FOUNDATION

5620 Morton Street
Philadelphia, PA 19144
☎ 215 849 3237

The Foundation publishes material on natural methods of birth control and provides information on communal groups. Their facilities include a printing service and they do have a small airplane! Training is given in offset printing.

Publications: 'The Natural Birth Control Book'; ARF Newsletter.

CALIFORNIA INSTITUTE OF TRANSPERSONAL PSYCHOLOGY
250 Oak Grove Avenue
Menlo Park, California 94025
☎ 415 326 1960

CITP offers a PhD degree in Transpersonal Psychology. This includes two years of clinical, social, theoretical, physical and spiritual study. There is also an internship phase and a dissertation project. CITP's goal is to provide a well-balanced integrated programme which facilitates personal growth and spiritual unfoldment.

Publication: 'Peak Experience', school newsletter, weekly during classes.

CONSCIOUS LIVING FOUNDATION
PO Box 513 E
Manhattan, Kansas 66502
☎ 913 539 2449

The Foundation is concerned with research and education on self-regulation. They publish English, Spanish and German cassettes, books and equipment for stress management, biofeedback and relaxation. Free catalogue.

THE EINSTEIN ACADEMY
34 Manomet Avenue
Hull, MA 02045
☎ 518 794 7515

The Academy's services are based around the teachings of Sufi Hazrat Inayat Khan.

Publication: 'Talks by an American Sufi'.

FOUR DIRECTIONS INC.
608 N. Douglas Street
Los Angeles, California 90026
☎ 213 620 1095

Four Directions is a spiritual non-profit organization and was created to fulfil the vision of walking in balance with our Mother Earth by preserving and implementing the traditional teachings left to us by our ancestors.

Four Directions is the first organization of its kind offering services for urban people who are seeking alternatives for a better way of life for themselves and for our Mother Earth. We primarily offer services conceived from the teachings of our Creator and our ancestors to help those who feel alienated and hopeless about their social and living situations.

Publications: Several books on Sioux teachings.

THE INTERNATIONAL INSTITUTE OF INTEGRAL HUMAN SCIENCES
PO Box 1387
Station H, Montreal
Quebec H3G 2N3, Canada
☎ 514 937 8359

The Institute is concerned with New Age and holistic education, parapsychology, psychic research and comparative religion. Many workshops and conferences are held and degree programmes in conjunction with the World University of Ojai, California are offered.

Publication: Newsletter for members.

LORIAN ASSOCIATION
PO Box 147
Middleton, WI 53562
☎ 608 833 0455

Lorian is a spiritually oriented educational association whose aim is to serve the emergence of a new planetary culture.

Publication: 'Revelation: The Birth of a New Age', David Spangler; 'To Hear the Angels Sing', Dorothy Maclean; 'Conversations with John' (booklet); Three Songbooks by the New Troubadours.

MARK-AGE INC.
5555 SW 64th Avenue
Fort Lauderdale, Florida 33314
☎ 315 587 5555

Mark-Age is a spiritual educational organization teaching the Second Coming of Christ awareness for all on Earth and of Christ Jesus (Sananda) as Prince of Earth. As a focus for Hierarchal Board, Mark-Age has five divisions: Healing Haven; University of Life; Mark-Age Meditations (MAM); Mark-Age Information-Nations (MAIN); Centers of Light.

Publications: MAIN (Mark-Age Inform-Nations) magazine; Healing Haven Journal.

NAROPA INSTITUTE
1111 Pearl Street
Boulder, Colorado 80302
☎ 303 444 0202

Naropa Institute is a small, non-sectarian college developed by Chogyam Trungpa Rinpoche, Tibetan Buddhist master of meditation. For seven years it has offered programmes in the performing arts, psychology, Buddhist Studies, science and education. All of these programmes are experientially oriented and aimed not merely at the academic training of students, but also for their personal growth and self-discovery. Students are taught to unite intellect and intuition through the actual practice of the field they are studying. Courses at Naropa are open to the student seeking degrees, as well as anyone who desires a provocative learning environment for the study of dance, poetics, music, theatre, martial arts, Buddhist studies, policial psychology, science or education.

Publications: 'Naropa Institute Bulletin'; 'Psychology Journal'; Catalogue.

OMEGA INSTITUTE FOR HOLISTIC STUDIES
Box 571
Lebanon Springs, New York 12114
☎ 518 794 8850

Omega Institute is a not-for-profit educational organization which has gained an international reputation for its innovative programmes in the many fields of holistic education. Provocative leaders from a wide variety of disciplines have included George Leonar, Elisabeth Kubler-Ross, Linus Pauling, Paul Winter Consort, Robert Bly, Marilyn Ferguson, and a host of others. Omega offers a chance for participants to study with an outstanding faculty in a beautiful country setting.

Publication: Omega Institute Summer Program Brochure (spring).

SCHOOL OF LIVING
RD 7 York
Pennsylvania 17402
☎ 717 755 2666

A membership organization for re-education of adults in defining and solving major, universal problems of living.

Publication   Quarterly 'Green Revolution'.

SPIRITUAL HIERARCHY INFORMATION CENTRE INC.
2220 N. 47th Avenue
Hollywood Hills, Florida 33021
☎ 305 966 7272

The Centre publishes teachings and offers lecture programmes concerned with the White Brotherhood and the I Am Presence. Correspondence is the main method of teaching but meditation facilities are available.

THOMAS JEFFERSON RESEARCH CENTER
1143 North Lake Avenue
Pasadena, California 91104
☎ 213 798 0791

Research and development of programmes designed to solve human problems, especially leadership development, motivation, character development, character rehabilitation and parent training.

Publication: TJRC Research Letter.

UNITED FOCUS
PO Box 5019
Seattle, Washington 98105
☎ 206 632 6670

United Focus works towards the implementation of holistic teaching methods. It is concerned with transformation and futurism.

Publication: 'Esoteric Psychology'.

UNITY OF KNOWLEDGE PUBLICATIONS
618 26th Street South
Arlington, Virginia 22202
☎ 703 684 8993

Unity of Knowledge publish and distribute books pertaining to the Oneness of Life and the Unity of Knowledge.

Publications: 'The Oneness of Life' (book); 'Creed for Aquarius' (pamphlet in verse).

USA COMMUNICATIONS
(Fred Anthony Warren, Editor)
3760 Wesson
Detroit, Michigan 48210
☎ 313 895 5981

USA Communications is a Newsletter and a Switchboard (one of many) serving the New Age Unity Consciousness. It shifts information from group to group for consideration without judgment but with discernment in the Inner Crystal Consciousness realizing that there are many 'levels of truth' each valid in relation to its own frame-of-reference!

Projects of USA Communications:

1 Switchboard for New Age Groups.

2 Publicizes the New Age Government 'Blueprint' received from higher levels of consciousness called the 'Unified States of Awareness'.

3 Brain Trust for Free Energy – a grass roots association of citizens who collect and circulate data showing that there are many alternate free-energy inventions which have been blocked by the vested interests of the world. A public relations thrust, hoping to influence sleeping-mass-consciousness to become awake and to take its own responsibility in a world-wide self-government. (Shades of the New Age hopes!)

4 Linking of Lights – mutual working together among individuals and groups, based on the principle that 'energy follows thought' and that a world thought-form of energy for good can be built up.

5 Peace Colleges – fosters same.

6 The Academy For The Open Book of Cosmic History – since the earth is roughly 4 billion years old, and mankind has been on earth for at least $18^{1}/_{2}$ million years, the AOBCH feels the 'lost history' may be retrieved, difficult though it may be!

7 Project Karma-lite (Carmelite) – attempts to release the stuck-energy-of-the-ages in the earth forcefield (the memory of all the negativities, wars, pogroms, civil wars) so that a positive forcefield of memories may be put in its place!

8 The Little School of St Francis – a holistic University in Spirit, practising harmlessness and love towards all levels of Life.

9 The Healing Order of the Emerald Cross.

10 The Church of the Inner Christ – by recognizing and acknowledging the inner-core-divinity of Everyman/woman, whether already resurrected or yet as potential, this ministry is in the action of healing of the mass consciousness false-self-image, hoping to replace it with one's true identity – each as a god, a co-creator with the collective divinity.

VINCENT SCHOOL AND INSTITUTE
1147 S. Robertson Boulevard
Los Angeles, California 90035
☎ 213 275 2498

The School specializes in holistic health education and runs courses in Swedish massage therapy and Ganzheit therapy. There is also a regular programme of lectures.

WORLD UNIVERSITY OF AMERICA
197 North Ventura Street
Ojai, California 93023
☎ 805 646 1444

World University is a private university, fully approved by the state of California, authorized to issue degrees in philosophy, psychology, world peace studies and ecumenical ministry.

Publications: Many books and articles by Dr Benito F. Reyes, President.

EUROPE

ASSOCIATION INTERNATIONALE POUR EDUCATION INTEGRÉE
(THE INTERNATIONAL ASSOCIATION FOR INTEGRATIVE EDUCATION)
CP 141
1225 Chêne-Bourg, Geneva, Switzerland
☎ 022 61 77 08

The IAIE is a small non-profit educational association that was formed in October 1979 under the Swiss Civil Code. The objective of the Association is the establishment of an international centre for integrative education as a project, in the first instance, in the field of continuing education. A programme of inter-disciplinary research, a summer school, lecture series and publications are also envisaged.

The Association is concerned with *integrative* education as they believe that it is the task of education to enable each human being to develop and integrate their potentialities and abilities, their knowledge and beliefs, their inner and outer experiences into personally and socially constructive patterns of life. The idea of integrative education belongs to all of those concepts of human life and learning that emphasize the 'whole' person.

Publications: 'The Geneva Centre'; 'The International Association for Integrative Education'; 'The IAIE Newsletter'.

EDIZIONI L'ETA' DELL' ACQUARIO
Via Vespucci 41
10129 Torino, Italy
☎ 011 5852 14

This is an Italian Centre dedicated to the Aquarian Age and the new plan of consciousness.

Publications: Several booklets. A guide to groups, published in the Italian language.

THE IONIC CENTRE
12 Strat
Syndesmou
Athens 136, Greece

The centre is concerned with scientific, cultural and spiritual studies with its central focus on Hellenic civilization, ancient and modern.

'LE JARDIN INTERIEUR'
(MUZ MURRAY (Ramana Baba))
Chemin des Peyrieres
Route de Vauvenarques
Les Trois Bons Dieux
13000 Aix-en-Provence, France
☎ 42 23 38 08

Muz Murray's work is the creation of a synthesis of spiritual experience and techniques, from all traditions (yet attached to none), in order to guide the seeker on the way best suited to himself. Thus my 'Way of Unlearning' is a simple 'Sharing of the Inner Quest' with fellow-travellers on the Way Within.

Publication: 'Seeking the Master – A Guide to the Ashrams of India'.

THE REST OF THE WORLD

BHARATA SHANGRI LA
161/2 Rajpur Road
Jakhan, Dehra Dun, India

Promotes the teaching of esoteric and exoteric truth and is concerned with raising the consciousness of humanity and the world, through truth of Self and God Realization. The teaching of Universal Brotherhood is mainly conducted through the post.

TAUHARA CENTRE
PO Box 125
Mapara Road, Acacia Bay,
Taupo, New Zealand
☎ 074 87 507

Tauhara is the expression of an unfolding vision. It was founded to create a spiritual and educational centre which would draw together people and groups of differing viewpoints and methods of working, but united in their search for truth and the establishment of goodwill and understanding in the world.

Tauhara is a free association of people from throughout New Zealand and beyond. Members come from all walks of life, all faiths and hold many diverse views. They come together to share and learn, to give and receive, working together physically, mentally and spiritually, thereby extending and enriching the expression of Tauhara. Fundamental to Tauhara's working is the vision of a free and loving network of people throughout the planet dedicated to the realization of the harmony within all creation.

4

SPIRITUAL TRADITIONS

INTRODUCTION
BY WINIFRED BREWIN

The religions of the world are the cultural manifestation of a central Truth and of a spiritual experience so basic that every society on earth has created a form for its expression. However, because of the differing stages in man's evolution and the differences in culture, in climate and environment, it is natural for each society to have developed, adapted or modified into differing formal expressions that which is, in essence, the same spiritual experience and the same underlying Truths.

There are two strands to every religion: the inner, esoteric aspect consists of the foundational Truth found at the heart of all spiritual faiths. The one Truth – existing 'in the beginning' – is that there is one God of all mankind – a God of 'love'. The goal of all the religions of the world, throughout all time, has been to help or teach man to experience, in mind and heart, that 'love' of God and to express that sense of union, at-one-ment or yoga (as it is called in several religious faiths) in practical, intelligent and lighted ways in the world of daily living so that the 'brotherhood' of man becomes a factual reality. The other strand in the world religions is concerned with the method or system which is designed to help man arrive at the experience of a 'God of love'. This is the more obvious outer, institutionalized aspect of the religions, and the dogmas, doctrines, rites and rituals of each religion differ according to the need and understanding of the people it is designed to help.

One of the central realities found at the heart of every religion is the universally recognized fact of God, the creator. It may be called by any name for It cannot be defined by names. But consciously or unconsciously, all men recognize God Transcendent and God Immanent. The Eastern faiths may have emphasized God Immanent, deep within the human heart, 'nearer than hands or feet', whereas the Western faiths may have concentrated on God Transcendent, outside His Universe, the Onlooker. But in Shri Krishna's beautiful statement in the Bhagavad Gita we find this universal truth expressed in both aspects: 'Having pervaded this whole universe with a fragment of Myself, I remain.'

Another common factor in all the world faiths is that of men's relationship to God as sons of a Father. Long before the followers of Jesus were taught to pray 'Our Father which art in Heaven', the Aryans of India addressed God as 'Father'.

Following on this Truth is the recognition of the brotherhood of man. The relationship of man, one to another, has been called 'brotherhood' and right down the ages and in all faiths brotherhood has been expressed as human fellowship and right human relations. The founders of all the world religions, without exception, have 'called' to their followers to live by this law of unity and brotherly love. In the words of the Lord Buddha, of Jesus and in the Vedas we find these almost identically worded teachings: 'With pure thoughts and fullness of love I will do toward others what I do for myself' – the Buddha. 'Do unto others what ye would have others do unto you.' 'Love thy neighbour as thyself' – Jesus Christ. And in the Vedas it is stated: 'Thou art That'. Zoroaster proclaims 'That which is good for all and anyone, for whomsoever – that is good for me. . . .' 'Do not do to others what ye do not wish done to yourself', is found in the Mahabharata.

This teaching on brotherhood could be called the 'doctrine of the heart'. It is the golden thread running through all the world religions and today the awakening of the 'heart' of man to a sense of responsibility for his brother, and to an expressed goodwill, is breaking down all barriers between religion and religion, race and race, and between the developed and the underdeveloped countries. Wherever 'the common good' of the human family is being worked for, be it in the social, cultural, economic, educational, scientific or political fields of relationship, there we can recognize the unifying 'heart doctrine' at work and the one God of love coming into expression in the world.

The fact of immortality and of eternal persistence is a truth that lies deep within the human heart. The religions of the world have all presented this fact even if there have been differing emphases at different times. The Eastern faiths teach the Law of Cause and Effect and of repeated incarnations until perfection is attained, whereas the Christian's interpretation has presented an image of immortality in a static Heaven and Hell. But in spite of the incomplete nature of our understanding at present, our eternal persistence is one of the foundational Truths presented in one form or another in all the world religions.

Common to all world religions is the continuity of the spiritual Revelation and the need of man for God and God for man. Never has Deity left Itself at any time without witness. Never has man demanded light but that the light has been forthcoming. Never has there been a time, cycle or world period when there was not the giving out of the teaching and spiritual help which human need demanded. Always, age after age, in answer to need, the Saviour, the Avatar or the World Teacher has issued forth and brought to man fresh revelation. These Teacher/Messengers come as founders of a new understanding of man's relationship to God and to each other. Their lives have been examples of a fresh expression of Godliness. Again and again, millennium after millennium, they have come forth to restore the Truth of a God of love. Particularly when the peoples have forgotten or ignored the brotherhood of man, when crime and evil, selfishness and chaos go beyond limits, then it is that They come forth to restore the Truth to common knowledge. They 'call' to a return to righteous living and to restore the 'doctrine of the heart' in order that man may fulfil the needs of society and live at peace and in goodwill and right relationships with his neighbour. And common to all religious traditions is the teaching of the fact that there is a path to God. In every race and nation, in every climate and every part of the world, and throughout the endless reaches of time itself, back into the limitless past, men and women have found that path to union or at-one-ment with God. They have trodden it and accepted its conditions, endured its disciplines, received its rewards and found their goal. Arrived there, they have 'entered into the joy of the Lord', participated in the mysteries of the kingdom of heaven, dwelt in the glory of the divine Presence, and then returned to the ways of men, to create a world in which the love of God works out as brotherhood and right human relations in the world of daily affairs.

UK

THE ANTHROPOSOPHICAL SOCIETY
35 Park Road
London W1
☎ 01 723 4400

The Society is the British headquarters for the teachings of Rudolf Steiner, the German mystic who explored from a practical viewpoint the occult sciences. Many of his teachings are oriented towards a mystical vision of Christianity but he also wrote in detail on the origins of man and the universe.

Lectures are given every Tuesday evening on aspects of Rudolf Steiner's teachings and work. The Society also holds weekly painting, drama and speech classes. More intensive study classes are also run on a regular basis.

Publications: The Rudolf Steiner Press has made available the works of Steiner which are produced in many volumes.

ARICA INFORMATION SERVICE
57 Marlborough Mansions
Cannon Hill, London NW6
☎ 01 435 4142

Arica offers courses, self-study materials, and publications based on a comprehensive theory of human development, providing a practical method for achieving greater self-understanding, well being, and awareness. Arica courses reduce stress, improve health, and develop greater resources of energy and strength to deal with the complexities of modern life.

Publications: There are several books and papers by Oscar Ichazo.

THE ATLANTEANS
Runnings Park
Croft Bank
West Malvern
Worc WR14 4BP

The Atlanteans seek to understand life and the spiritual forces that motivate the universe. The wisdom of the Atlanteans comes from an esoteric source and was originally published in seven booklets which form the foundation to their work. The activities of the Atlanteans also encompasses healing and meditation, the occult and psychic development.

They hold regular meetings in this country and abroad and now plan to hold weekend and one-day courses on healing, meditation and natural health.

Publications: Bi-monthly magazine – 'The Atlantean'. Also 'The Atlantean Manual' which is a course in meditation. Other books are available containing the group's esoteric teachings.

AXMINSTER LIGHT CENTRE
66 Willhayes Park
North Street, Axminster, Devonshire, EX13 5QW
☎ 0297 32094

This is a teaching centre receiving information important to our times from higher sources, such as teachers from the inner planes and outer space. The teachings are sent to others through the post with the desire of increasing knowledge and understanding. They include important ideas as to the spiritual nature of man and the world changes we are now experiencing.

Publications: The Omega Papers, newsletters, quarterly papers on specified subjects, leaflets.

BESHARA
Sherborne Stables
Sherborne, Cheltenham, Glos.
☎ 045 088 292

Beshara offers programmes which consist of practical work, meditation, study of mystical texts and Zikr or rememoration. Since the school is founded on the principle of the Unity or essential Oneness of existence, no activity is given particular priority, rather the aim is to establish a single and constant awareness.

Beshara offers short and long residential courses in intensive esoteric education and can provide a good deal of information on the esoteric and mystical tradition.

Beshara also runs courses at Chisholme House, Roberton, Hawick, Roxburgshire.

Publications: Occasional newsletter; translations of the works of 'Ibn Arabi' and other writings.

BRITISH BUDDHIST ASSOCIATION
57 Farringdon Road
London, EC1
☏ 01 242 5538

The association is primarily concerned with the arrangement of courses, programmes and evening classes at colleges for the serious student of Buddhism.

BUDDHIST SOCIETY
58 Eccleston Square
London SW1
☏ 01 828 1313

The Society runs many courses, lecture programmes and meetings on all aspects of Buddhism. The Society has also made available a reading room, library, bookstore, meditation room and can provide information on the Buddhist path.

Publications: Regular programme of events.

CHURCHES FELLOWSHIP FOR PSYCHICAL & SPIRITUAL STUDIES
St Mary Abchurch
Abchurch Lane
London EC4
☏ 01 626 0306

The Fellowship has branches in other parts of the country and is concerned with the study and investigation of all forms of psychic and spiritual phenomena. Its aim is to show the relevance of such research to the Christian faith.

Publication: Magazine – 'The Christian Parapsychologist'.

THE CHRISTIAN COMMUNITY
Temple Lodge
51 Queen Caroline Street
London, W6 9QL
☏ 01 748 8388

The Christian Community, based around the ideas of Rudolf Steiner, is concerned with Christian studies and ritual. They also operate counselling services.

Publications: Several books including those by Rudolf Steiner.

DHARMA STUDY GROUP LONDON
(part of VAJRADHATU organization)
74 Tantallon Road
London SW12
☎ 01 673 6115

The group is involved with the practice and study of Buddha dharma as taught by the Vajracarya the Venerable Chögyam Trungpa Rinpoche – a dharma master currently residing in the West. Great emphasis is laid on the practice of meditation.

Publications: Regular newsletter. A booklet and information sheet on the group is also available.

DZOGCHEN ORGYEN CHO LING
76 Princess Road
London NW6
☎ 01 624 8246

This is one of London's main Tibetan Buddhist meditation and study centres, founded by Sogyal Rinpoche. The centre offers courses and lectures on aspects of Tibetan Buddhism and is well known for its visiting Lamas.

Publications: Newsletter and programme of events.

FRIENDS OF THE WESTERN BUDDHIST ORDER
51 Roman Road
Bethnal Green
London E2 0HU
☎ 01 981 1225

This is the head office of the Order and is also a community structured around the Buddhist system. The FWBO also have many other community operations in other parts of the country and abroad and full details can be obtained from the above address. Those who live in the communities are committed to personal enlightenment through work, study, meditation and the arts.

The Order runs several business enterprises which include printing, wholefood co-operatives, design, building and vegetarian cafés.

Publication: Friends of the Western Buddhist Order newsletter.

THE GATEKEEPERS TRUST
160 Maryland Road
London N22

The trust was founded to investigate and experience the mysteries of the earth seen as a living spiritual organism, and is dedicated to the renewal of the earth by communication, research, pilgrimage, ritual and illumination. This activity has begun to reveal the vital importance of experiencing the earth as a living temple, and the landscape as a kingdom of lesser temples, described by, and visible to the sensitive as an architecture of living etheric forms, power centres in the landscape, waiting only for the light of human consciousness to burst forth again into renewed life appropriate for our times and tasks. The Trust organizes pilgrimages in this country and abroad.

Publications: Several booklets are planned for publication.

THE GENERAL CONFERENCE OF THE NEW CHURCH
20 Bloomsbury Way
London WC1A 2TH
☎ 01 242 8574

Making available the teachings of Emanuel Swedenborg, the great revelator of the spiritual world and interpreter of the Bible, through publications, lectures and courses. They also offer detailed information about life after death and New Age theology.

Publications: 'Lifeline' (monthly); Quarterly newsletter and 'New Church' Magazine.

KAGYU SAMYE-LING TIBETAN CENTRE
Eskdalemuir
Nr Langholm, Dumfriesshire, Scotland
☎ 05416 232

Kagyu Samye-Ling is primarily a Buddhist centre. It aims to provide study and meditation facilities for Buddhists and non-Buddhists alike, in order to help increase mental and spiritual well-being in the world. It is a place where different kinds of people can find quiet and retreat. The centre holds several courses on the Tibetan tradition.

Publications: Translations of Tibetan Buddhist prayers and texts.

LECTORIUM ROSICRUCIANUM
International School of the Golden Rosycross
BM LR7
London WC1V 6XX

The Lectorium Rosicrucianum proclaims the existence of a path of Liberation from this fallen world, a path taught in the ancient Mystery Schools and more recently by the Cathars, Templars and classical Rosicrucians. As a modern Christo-centric Mystery School, it aims to help its pupils actually to follow this path to its end.

The School, with its headquarters in Holland, operates in most European cities and also in North and South America, Africa and New Zealand. Regular public lectures are held in London, but there is no centre here as yet.

Publications: More than 30 books are available in several languages covering all areas of their field of study.

THE LIVING QABALAH
(Will Parfitt)
42 Corringham Road
London NW 11
☎ 01 458 2537

The Living Qabalah unfolds the methods of Western esotericism in a practical and relevant way through individual tuition, groups, courses and training for the whole person in the Qabalah, Tree of Life and the Tarot.

Publications: Free brochure on application; papers, articles, etc. for trainees.

LODGE OF THE STAR
57 Warescot Road
Brentwood, Essex CM15 9HH

Lodge of the Star is an esoteric group offering healing facilities, creative meditation and revealed teachings. The Lodge's teacher, an Elder Brother of the race, is the guiding light, and through his guidance important teachings for the New Age are being received. The Lodge is linked to the Brotherhood of the Star and its work at this time is to aid in the manifestation of Christ Consciousness within humanity. The Lodge offers all its services to the public and its main outpouring is through healing and the distribution of the teachings. Healing here is both individual and planetary in scope.

Publications: A regular newsletter containing up-to-date news and teachings; a cassette tape recording of revealed ideas and insights.

LONDON SUFI CENTRE FOR HOLISTIC STUDIES

58 St Stephens Gardens
London W2
☎ 01 221 3215

This is a growing centre of the international Sufi Order of the West, linked to Hazrat Inayat Khan and Pir Vilayat Inayat Khan. The Sufi Order honours all religions, traditions and teachers. Its broadest aim is the unity of mankind in brotherhood and wisdom, achieved through tolerance, compassion and respect for freedom.

The Centre offers esoteric studies, meditation, spiritual healing, practical spirituality, sacred dance and holistic theatre facilities.

Publication: Quarterly newsletter.

THE LONDON STUDY GROUP OF THE ROSICRUCIAN FELLOWSHIP

26 Pretoria Avenue
Walthamstow, London E17 7DE
☎ 01 521 9366

The Rosicrucian Fellowship is an association of Christians established for the purpose of helping to make Christianity a living factor in the world. Its teachings give a definite, logical and sequential explanation of the origin, evolution and future development of the world and man, from both the spiritual and scientific aspects.

The Fellowship provides healing and spiritual counselling and offers correspondence courses in the Rosicrucian philosophy, astrology and Bible study. However, these courses are only available from the Fellowship headquarters at PO box 713, Oceanside, California 92054, USA.

Publications: Various books by Max Heindel and a monthly magazine.

LUCIS TRUST

Suite 54
3 Whitehall Court
London SW1A 2EF
☎ 01 839 4512

The establishing of right human relations is the overall objective of the service activities of the Lucis Trust – the Arcane School, Triangles and World Goodwill. A wide range of literature and regular newsletters are available free of charge. The Lucis Press publishes the 24 books by Alice A. Bailey.

MANJUSHRI INSTITUTE – London

14c Oseney Crescent
Kentish Town
London NW5 2AY
☎ 01 267 8929

The Institute is part of a worldwide network of Buddhist centres started by Lama Thubten Yeshe and Lama Zopa Rinpoche. It runs a large centre at Connishead Priory, Ulverston, Cumbria. The Institute offers courses on Tibetan Buddhism which include meditations. They are able to provide information on Buddhist philosophy and psychology.

Publications: These are known as the 'Wisdom Publications' which include many important texts.

ORDER OF MELCHISEDEK

BCM/ELADE
London WC1N 3XX

This is a small group offering free training to suitable persons desirous of freeing themselves from worldly systems and philosophies. This is the Road to spiritual Adeptship for work on an hierarchical basis.

The Order has many postal contacts and provides personal inner spiritual and mental development. Participation in all activities is by invitation only. The training programmes are always private and personal sessions are held.

Publications: Free literature is available.

ORDER OF THE CROSS

10 De Vere Gardens
London W8 5AE
☎ 01 937 7012

The New Age Message of the Order of the Cross is for souls seeking to recover the illumined state of Christ consciousness. Worship, meditation, creative arts, study of the Teachings of the founder, Rev. J. Todd Ferrier, make up the spiritual programme. All members are vegetarian/vegan. Enquirers are always welcome.

Publications: Writings of the founder.

THE RAJA YOGA CENTRE

98 Tennyson Road
London NW6 7SB
☎ 01 328 2478

Raja Yoga, a unique combination of meditation and study, has the effect of changing us, subtly and deeply, back into the pure beings we once were. Meditation is taught individually and in groups. Lectures, exhibitions, conferences, audio visuals, music and dance performances are arranged throughout the world. All services are free.

Publications: 'World Renewal' (monthly magazine); 'Purity' (monthly paper); a variety of books on meditation, spiritual knowledge and the Centre itself.

RESEARCH INTO LOST KNOWLEDGE ORGANISATION

36 College Court
Hammersmith
London W6

The organization is primarily involved with research into sacred geometry and architecture and the study of earth patterns and earth magic. They have researched ley lines, ancient landscapes, temples, standing stones, cathedrals etc . . .

Publications: Include 'Glastonbury – A study in patterns', 'Britain – A study in patterns'.

RIGPA

44 St Paul's Crescent
London NW1 9TN
☎ 01 485 4342

'Rigpa' means 'awakening wisdom'. The Rigpa Fellowship, a Registered Charity, is dedicated to exploring the teaching of Buddha in the context of modern life, directed by Venerable Lama Sogyal Rinpoche, meditation master and scholar from Tibet.

A complete three-year training, weekend seminars, evening teachings, retreats, and an annual summer school are available. The centre is visited by many eminent Buddhist teachers.

Publications: 'Face to Face' by Lama Sogyal Rinpoche; 'View, Meditation and Action' by Lama Sogyal Rinpoche; list of books by Indian and Western publishers available by mail order. Large tape-library of teachings by many eminent teachers.

SATYANANDA YOGA CENTRE

70 Thurleigh Road
London SW12
☎ 01 673 4869

The Centre holds regular classes in London using asanas, pranayamas and meditation, as taught by Swami Samananda Saraswati. Hatha Yoga classes are open to the public.

Publication: 'Yoga Times' has now ceased publication but it is hoped that the journal will be published in a different format at a later date.

SIVANANDA YOGA VEDANTA CENTRE

50 Chepstow Villas
London W11
☎ 01 229 7970

The Sivananda Yoga Centre is a non-profit, non-sectarian organization founded by Swami Vishnudevananda. Our purpose is to propagate the teachings of yoga to help individuals achieve health, happiness and inner peace. Our teachers offer classes emphasizing proper exercise, breathing, relaxation, diet and concentration and meditation as taught to them by Swami Vishnu. Courses are offered in beginner's yoga, beginner's meditation, pregnant and pre-pregnant yoga, fasting clinic, vegetarian cooking classes, Indian musical instrument tuition.

Publication: 'Sivananda'.

SPIRITUALIST ASSOCIATION OF GREAT BRITAIN

33 Belgrave Square
London, SW1
☎ 01 235 3351

This is the headquarters of the spiritualist movement in the UK with local branches in other parts of the country.

The Association in Belgrave Square runs a regular programme of lectures and psychic demonstrations, featuring the best mediums in the country. There is also a book store and a restaurant. The association can provide information to members on all aspects of spiritualism.

Publication: 'The Spiritualist Gazette'.

SRI CHINMOY CENTRE

16D Portland Road
London W11 4LA
☎ 01 727 9680

Meditation is the main activity of the Centre, under the spiritual guidance of Sri Chinmoy. Other important activities include sports, musical concerts, drama, poetry and public lectures and workshops.

Publications: Sri Chinmoy has written over 400 books on meditation and kindred subjects.

THE THEOSOPHICAL SOCIETY

50 Gloucester Place
London W1H 3HJ
☎ 01 935 9261

The Society encourages brotherhood, tolerance, freedom of belief and the search for truth. Theosophy is the essence of all religions, the Divine Wisdom concerning the origins and purpose of man and the universe. Members can meet in autonomous groups which form a network in over 60 countries.

The society was founded upon the teachings of H. P. Blavatsky received from the Masters of Wisdom and presented in the monumental work, 'The Secret Doctrine'.

Publications: The Theosophical publishing house produces many books on Theosophy and related areas. Journals: 'The Theosophist'; 'The Theosophical Journal'.

THROSSEL HOLE PRIORY

Carrshield
Nr Hexham, Northumberland, NE47 8AL
☎ 04985 204

Throssel Hole Priory is a training monastery, parish church and retreat centre following the Sōtō Zen Buddhist tradition. It was founded in 1972 by Rev. Rōshi Jiyu-Kennett, OBC, Abbess and Spiritual Director of Shasta Abbey, Headquarters of the Order of Buddhist Contemplatives of the Sōtō Zen Church.

Publication: 'Journal of Throssel Hole Priory', quarterly.

UNIVERSAL PEACE MISSION
75 Chesham Road
Amersham, Bucks
☎ 02403 6846

The aims of the Universal Peace Mission are:
(1) To bring together all religious institutions so that they can work for the common purpose of unity and peace in the world.
(2) To inspire men to respect all faiths by greater understanding of what each one teaches, so that there will be no divisions or 'isms', but a common ideal for humanity.
(3) To help mankind build up its life from within to create a better, more noble and prosperous life for all.
(4) To create a flood of cultural and spiritual movements which will bring about the liberation of life from suppression and exploitation.
(5) To discuss and explore the causes of the present-day global crisis.

Publication: 'Solace' magazine.

VIEWPOINT AQUARIUS
c/o Fish Tanks Ltd
49 Blandford Street
London W1
☎ 01 935 3719

Viewpoint Aquarius produce a magazine of the same name and are concerned with the teachings of H. P. Blavatsky, occult law, yoga, meditation and flying saucers.

THE WHITE EAGLE LODGE
New Lands
Rake, Liss, Hants. GU33 7HY
☎ 073082 3300

The Lodge is a spiritual school developing the understanding of the Christ in the heart of man. It is based upon the teachings of White Eagle who has presented teachings in a simple yet beautiful way. Services of worship, healing and meditation are held, most of which are open to the public. The Lodge also has a London centre at 9 St Mary Abbots Place, Kensington, London W8 6LS.

Publications: Many books on spiritual unfoldment. 'Stella Polaris' (bimonthly magazine).

NORTH AMERICA

ASSOCIATION OF SANANDA AND SANAT KUMARA INC.
\# 1 Vista – PO Box 35
Mt Shasta, California 96067
☎ 916 926 2316

The Association Sananda and Sanat Kumara, is both Exoteric and Esoteric in organization. The Exoteric aspect is known to the world of men as 'Association Sananda and Sanat Kumara, Inc.' or ASSK. This is the aspect whereby contact is made with those coming for counselling and spiritual help – also the mailing of the 'Holy Scripts' to those who ask for them, by sending in the 'Yellow Slips' by mail. The 'Gate House' and living quarters for staff, and the grounds, are part of the Exoteric aspect of ASSK. Within this Outer Organization is the 'Inner Temple', known as 'The Temple of Sananda and Sanat Kumara', which is the 'Esoteric' aspect of the Association, through which the Holy Scripts are received. The Outer and Inner aspects of this organization, both as to Name and Purpose, were organized under Instructions and Guidance of The Great and Mighty Council, of Which The Lord God Sananda is Head.

ASTARA, INC.
800 W. Arrow Highway, PO Box 5003
Upland, Ca 91786
☎ 714 981 4941

Astara is a center of all religions and philosophies, a school of the ancient mysteries and an institute of psychic research.

THE BEAR TRIBE
Medicine Society
PO Box 9167
Spokone, WA 99209
☎ 509 258 7755

The Bear Tribe is an inter-racial group concerned with the North American spiritual tradition, preparing for vision, self-reliance, vision quests, apprenticeships, ceremonies and tribal lifestyles. They are also mail-order book distributors and hold various events in the USA and Europe on native American subjects and Earth Awareness.

Publications: 'Earth Awareness' magazine; Books: 'Buffalo Hearts', 'Bear Tribe Self Reliance Book'.

JEMEZ BODHI MANDALA

PO Box 8
Jemez Springs, NM 87025
☎ 505 829 3854

This is a Rinzai Zen Buddhist Retreat Center for individuals, couples or families. They run Zen practice introductory weekends and week-long intensive retreats.

Publication: Quarterly newsletter.

KARMA TRIYANA DHARMACHAKRA

352 Mead Mountain Road
Woodstock, New York 12498
☎ 914 679 2487

Karma Triyana Dharmachakra is a Tibetan Buddhist monastery and retreat centre situated in a remote area of the Catskill Mountains. It is a facility where highly realized Tibetan lamas give teachings on Buddhist philosophy and practical meditation instruction. Karma Triyana Dharmachakra is the main seat in North America of His Holiness Gyalwa Karmapa.

Publication: 'Densal', quarterly newsletter.

KESHAVASHRAM INTERNATIONAL CENTER

Box 260
Warrenton, Virginia 22186
☎ 703 347 9009

The first Hindu Temple was inaugurated in the USA by this Center. Current emphasis is on the science of words or the ancient Hindu tradition of meditation, using Vedic mantras.

NEW AGE TEACHINGS

37 Maple Street, Box 346
Brookfield, Massachusetts 01506–0346
☎ 617 867 3754

New Age Teachings is primarily a main ministry. They also conduct meditations, classes in awareness and have an open center for use by New Age groups.

Publication: 'New Age Teachings'.

MEDITATION GROUP – NEW YORK
40 East 49th Street, Suite 1903
New York, NY 10017
☎ 212 755 3027

The Group holds monthly meditation meetings at the time of the full moon to invoke an inflow of spiritual energies for humanity.

PRISON-ASHRAM PROJECT OF THE HANUMAN FOUNDATION
Rt 1, Box 201–N
Durham, North Carolina
☎ 919 493 3023

The Prison-Ashram Project serves to provide materials, advice and workshops, for people who are institutionalized or who work in institutions.

Publication: 'Inside-Out: A Spiritual Manual for Prison Life'.

SOCIETY OF PRAGMATIC MYSTICISM
Route 30
Pawlet, VT 05761
☎ 802 325 3107

The Society runs training programmes on mysticism through the post. Printed material is available by subscriptions or through the purchase of single volumes.

THE SUFI ORDER
1570 Pacheco Street
Sante Fe, New Mexico 87501
☎ 505 988 4411

The Sufi Order is a non-profit organization dedicated to the following: studying from an unbiased standpoint the teachings and methods of esoteric and mystical schools attached to the world religions, the organization of social welfare and educational programmes to promote mutual tolerance, understanding, co-operation and the spirit of universal brotherhood amongst all the people of the world, offering meditation instruction and seminars to the public, and giving spiritual training to its members. The leader of the Sufi Order is Pir Vilayat Inayat Khan.

Publications: 'The Message', monthly magazine; books of the teachings of Hazrat Inayat Khan, Pir Vilayat Inayat Khan, and others.

SYDA FOUNDATION

PO Box 600
S. Fallsburg, New York 12779
☎ 914 434 2000

The Foundation provides facilities throughout the world where people can learn and practise the teachings of Siddha Yoga as taught by Swami Muktananda.

Publication: 'The Siddha Path', a monthly journal of Siddha Yoga.

TRUTH CONSCIOUSNESS

Gold Hill, Salina Star Route
Boulder, Colorado 80302
☎ 303 449 7660

Swami Amar Jyoti created ashrams and community centers for seekers desiring spiritually centered lives under his guidance, places where aspirants can grow consciously toward enlightenment, in harmony with nature's laws. Centers operate within Truth Consciousness in America and Ananda Niketan in India. Satsangs, meditation, retreats and publications are offered.

EUROPE

ANTHROPOSOPHICAL SOCIETY

Boslaan 12
Zeist
Holland

The Anthroposophical Society in Holland not only provides information on the evolutionary and spiritual teachings of Rudolf Steiner but also offers help and assistance on Steiner's method of biodynamic agriculture and care of the human body and hygiene in general.

BHEDANTA

Fosdalgaard
9460 Brovst
Denmark

This school is located within pleasant surroundings on an old Danish farm. Their programme incorporates several spiritual disciplines and a vegetarian diet is adhered to. Bhedanta belongs to the Nordenfjord World University which serves as an education focus for the whole man.

Publication: 'Physiognomy' (NWU).

CENTRE VEDANTIQUE
Chemin des Gravannes 9
CH-1246 Corsier/GE, Switzerland
☏ 022 51 22 24

This is a branch of the Ramakrishna Mission with headquarters at Belur Math, Calcutta. Lectures are given (in French) by the Swami and other experts on Vedanta and comparative religion and philosophy; spiritual guidance and meditation by appointment.

Publications: In French; 'Science du Yoga Vol I and II', 'Actualité des Upanishads', 'Le Chemin de la Perfection'; in English, Italian as well as French: 'Myths and Symbols in Indian Civilization'.

KRISHNAMURTI FOUNDATION
c/o Barbino
Via di Montoro 8
Rome, Italy

The Foundation supports the work of Krishnamurti through lecture programmes on his ideas and also through publications.

MARTINUS INSTITUTE
Mariendalsvej 94/96
Copenhagen, Denmark
☏ 346280

The works of Martinus, his books and lectures are available through the Institute. All aspects of life are cosmically and logically analysed. Workshops and lectures in the English language are given every July and accommodation is available to visitors.

Publication: 'Kosmos' magazine.

ORAANSOUJELIJAT
(Protectors of the New Bud)
Korkeavuorenkatu 3C
SF-00140
Helsinki, Finland
☏ 179212

This New Age organization relates its function to the sweeping aside of dogmas and the promotion of a more natural and harmonious way of life.

SCANDINAVIAN YOGA AND MEDITATION SCHOOL

34013 Hamneda
Sweden
☎ 0372 55063

The School teaches yoga, tantra and meditation through various courses held in Sweden and other parts of the world. These are residential and include a four-year yoga and meditation teacher training.

Publication: 'Bindu' (English-language magazine).

SUFI ORDER CAMP DES AIGLES

14 Rue de la Tuilerie
92150 Suresnes
France

A Sufi camp is held every year with meditation instruction given by Pir Vilayat Khan, head of the Sufi Order of the West.

REST OF THE WORLD

BIHAR SCHOOL OF YOGA

Monghyr
Bihar 911201, India
☎ Monghyr 2334

The School aims to initiate aspiring individuals into yoga and to promote and make available a practical system of yogic education. The School consists of the Sivananda Ashram and a new ashram complex. It provides general yoga training, teacher training courses, kriya yoga courses, yoga therapy courses, etc.

Publications: Many Hindi and English books and a monthly yoga magazine.

BUDDHIST PUBLICATION SOCIETY

PO Box 61
Kandy, Sri Lanka
☎ 08 3679

The Buddhist Publication Society Inc. (founded 1958) publishes authentic literature on many aspects of Buddhist teaching and its practical application to life. Many general, specialized booklets and translations of Buddhist texts are available in the Wheel Series. Other specialized treatises bear on some particular aspect of Buddhism when compared with beliefs and attitudes common to the West or concepts of Western religions.

A comprehensive library of Buddhist literature has already been published in the Wheel Series-281 issues to date December 1981. Smaller booklets dealing with many different aspects of Buddhism are available in Bodhi Leaves series, 88 issues to date December 1981. Contributions to both are written by representative Buddhist scholars. These publications now circulate in 78 countries throughout the world.

THE CENTRAL INSTITUTE FOR KUNDALINI RESEARCH
14 Karan Nagar
Srinagar, Kashmir, India
☎ 73640

The Institute's activity is to promote objective research into Kundalini as the psycho-somatic mechanism working in the human frame responsible for man's evolution and the source of creativity, genius, psychic phenomena, mystical experience and certain forms of insanity. The institute conducts investigations of volunteer participants (by invitation only) in efforts to awaken Kundalini.

Mr Gene Kieffer, KRI, 475 Fifth Avenue, New York, NY 10017, USA and Miss Margaret Kobelt, KRF, Gemsenstrasse 7, 8006 Zurich, Switzerland can provide literature, cassettes, video tapes and speak at outside functions.

Publication: 'Kundalini', quarterly publication.

INDIAN INSTITUTE OF WORLD CULTURE
6 Shri B P Wadia Road, Post Box 402
Bangalore 560 004, India
☎ 0812 602581

Founded in 1945, the Institute owes its existence to the inspiration provided by the ideal of universal brotherhood. It is a non-sectarian, non-political, private, voluntary organization registered in Bangalore with the objective of promoting human brotherhood and culture. Its activities comprise holding talks, seminars, exhibitions, performances of dance, drama, music, maintaining a library of about 35,000 volumes essentially on culture, a separate children's library with about 8,000 volumes and a reading room which receives about 400 journals and periodicals from all over the world.

Publications: Monthly bulletin; 'Transactions', four times a year; Annual Report, books and pamphlets.

INTERNATIONAL ASSOCIATION FOR RELIGION AND PARAPSYCHOLOGY
(President: Hiroshi Motoyama, PhD)
4-11-7 Inokashira
Mitaka-Shi, Tokyo 181, Japan
☏ 0422 48 3535

The Association carries out research on the connections between science and religion, especially the subtle energy systems of the body and psychic phenomena, using sensitive devices especially designed by Dr Motoyama, as well as other traditional transducers. It also provides oriental and occidental diagnosis and treatment of physical and mental illness, as well as giving instruction in hatha and kundalini yoga.

Publications: Bi-monthly newsletter; 'Research for Religion and Parapsychology', twice- or thrice-yearly journal.

KARMA KAGYU TRUST
PO Box 15
New Bethesda 6286, South Africa

The Trust offers Buddhist study, meditation and retreats at its centre, which can accommodate 20 people at present. They can provide information on Buddhist meditation, bonsai and pottery, and are closely allied to other Buddhist groups.

SCIENTIFIC LIFE DIVINE MISSION
(Founder-Director Dr Ujjal Kumar Dutt, MSc, MDH)
58 Creek Row
Calcutta, 700014, India
☏ CAL 26 1648

The Mission is primarily concerned with the Divine Truths and Wisdom which can be found at the centre of all religions. Through the publication of various teachings concerned with meditation, brotherhood, reincarnation etc. the Mission helps to increase knowledge and understanding and above all unity between faiths and nations.

The group is non-political and seeks to explain the ancient truths using a scientific approach.

There are many publications available and those interested should write sending return postage if possible.

VIVEKANANDA KENDRA
Vivekanandapuram (PO), PC 629702
Districk-Kanyakumari
Tamil Nadu, India
☎ 61 50 32

A spiritually oriented service mission whose motto is 'Serve Man, Serve God'. This is the All-India headquarters which has 50 branch centres in India. The Centre, based on the teachings of Swami Vivekananda, offers yoga and meditation training and study through residential retreats.

Publications: Several books and booklets on Indian philosophy.

WAT BUDDHARANGSEE
88 Stanmore Road
Stanmore
New South Wales
2048 Australia
☎ 51 2039

This is a centre for the Theravada Buddhist tradition and teaching. Meditation retreat facilities available.

5

NEW AGE
COMMUNITIES

INTRODUCTION
BY FRANÇOIS DUQUESNE

Community is traditionally the birthplace of culture. Ancient and modern civilizations were seeded out of a rich welter of religious brotherhoods, pioneers' settlements and strategically placed communities that later flowered into villages and full-grown cities. It is within community that new values, ideals and lifestyles are being conceived and explored. It is community that gives meaning and coherence to culture. It is like the bamboo that helps the young sapling grow straight.

Why such a privileged place? Because it is in the simplicity of beginnings that ordering principles are more easily discerned. There are three relationships which any community needs to establish: firstly, to its natural environment, secondly to itself and thirdly to evolution. Like any living being it functions in space, time and consciousness. It is along these three axes that the whole of civilization will eventually develop. The choices and attitudes of a community in those three areas spell out the epistemological premises for the later establishment of its economic, socio-political and cultural networks.

Cultures, like communities are born, grow, decline and die. The forces of renewal are contained within the seeds. These are released when the over-ripe fruit falls from the tree and returns to the earth. In the dialectics of history the seed impulse for new culture always comes from the periphery. When the city is corrupt, prophets and seers return to the desert and the mountain, to receive a new vision of the purpose of evolution. Abraham left Ur, Jesus was born in a stable, and the Buddha left the palace in search of enlightenment. When the main culture has lost sight of its founding values and sense of direction, when these are no longer sufficient to provide meaning and fulfilment, one can observe migrations towards the margin, towards the uncluttered areas where once again, in the simplicity of new beginnings, the essential values are recovered. The cultural transformations of Western Europe, during the Middle Ages, the Renaissance and the Industrial Revolution for instance, were accompanied by the rise of religious, artistic or humanitarian communities that either spearheaded or resisted such changes. Monasteries and cathedrals were examples of the birth of new vision and creativity in the midst of the decaying feudal systems of Europe. When in the nineteenth century, the industrial revolution threatened to tear both natural and social landscapes apart, a wave of utopian communities and socialist philosophers (Owens, Fourrier, Saint Simon, etc.) arose to protest and counteract the excesses of the new technological materialism. Though many failed, they were none the less catalysts in the movement that since then has constantly been working for the creation of a more equitable social order.

The function of community then is to be a cradle for ideas and values that need to be incorporated in the dominant culture. Communities are laboratories where strategies for the survival and evolution of our species are being devised and experimented with. In our times, when the main industrial civilization seems unable to resolve the formidable crises that it has helped to precipitate, once again we see hundreds of thousands of people withdrawing their allegiance from central institutions, and fleeing to subcultures which, like new blades of green grass appearing in the cracks of a concrete jungle, are quietly blooming in civilization's own backyard.

The new communities have emerged in response to a need to revise culture. Those who have been successful have often had a spiritual commitment at their core coupled with an outward service orientation. Collectively they are giving birth to a set of values that may form a viable alternative to mainstream directions. The movement as a whole reaches deep into the question of 'how will 10 billion human beings be able to live at peace with themselves and the earth in but two or three generations?' Each community seeks to create a lifestyle that begins to be part of the solution. Often values such as 'voluntary simplicity', 'living lightly', caring, sharing, reverence for life and work as prayer, form the basis of their attitude towards the earth, humanity and the inner worlds of spirit.

Some experiment with appropriate technologies, others build with concrete and use computers in their work. Whatever their predilection, they all share a commitment to living in harmony and to personal and social renewal. Their vision of culture is one that encourages a maximum diversity and richness of expression. This apparent multiplicity does not mean a return to the parochialism of the pre-industrial village. Unity is created out of the spirit that connects them to humankind and to nature's eco-systems. They are often planetary in their outlook.

The communities described in this book have pledged themselves to a vision of rebirth, to the great spiritual transformation of our times. As such they will continue to grow and be a force of inspiration for the rest of the culture. It is only when they lose sight of the purpose that binds them to the whole that they are in danger of drifting into the by-waters of history. This is also the time when the negative, reactionary side of community may raise its head. The wilderness is the home of both the prophet and the madman. By being unconventional, out on a limb of the tree of culture, communities expose themselves to greater dangers at the same time they avail themselves of greater opportunities.

Not everyone has to migrate to a subculture. We have to remember that 75 per cent of the 4.5 billion human beings who are presently on the earth live in villages. The planet cannot support a global lifestyle that is 90 per cent concentrated in megalopolises. The communities of this book, most of them situated in the Western industrialized part of the world, are an attempt to re-validate, even to re-sacralize the small- to medium-size cultural unit of the village. As we move inexorably into a new world period, into an age that will have to combine the conquest of the atom with the harnessing of sun and wind, space colonies with compost-making, power with wisdom, the planetary with the vernacular, these new communities may well become the signposts on the road to our individual and species destiny.

UK

ALTERNATIVE COMMUNITIES MOVEMENT
18 Garth Road
Bangor, Gwynedd, N. Wales

The Movement seeks to encourage people to join or to build communities internationally. The purpose of this is to effect a more efficient international society since communities have the advantages of (a) economic and ecological stability, (b) socio/sexual/educational stability and (c) greater social stability.

ATLANTIS
Burtonport
Co. Donegal, Eire
Burtonport 30

Atlantis is a self-sufficient vegetarian commune on the north-east coast of Donegal. They practise primal therapy as a way of understanding the course of problems.

Publications: Many books and articles are available.

THE FINDHORN FOUNDATION
The Park
Forres IU36 OT2, Scotland
☎ 03098 72288

Findhorn is a community of two hundred permanent members dedicated to working out new ways of living and working together in which the divine essence of people, nature, tools and materials is given its proper importance. Findhorn is also an important educational and communications centre with a vision of a New Age.

There are guest programmes and workshops throughout the year covering many spiritual areas. Findhorn has a resource centre with information on related groups throughout the world.

Publications: There is a full range of books and tapes available. The community's magazine is 'Onearth'.

LOWER ROCKES
Compton Street
Butleigh, Glastonbury, Somerset
☎ 0458 50737

Lower Rockes is a small community providing individual sessions on healing, massage, acupressure, therapy, astrology, etc. They hold week-end workshops on self-awareness, dreams and co-counselling.

Publication: Bi-monthly programme.

LOWER SHAW FARM
Shaw
Nr Swindon, Wiltshire
☎ 0793 771080

A community offering residential facilities to groups of up to 30 people. The Farm offers services in organic gardening, yoga, arts and crafts and animal husbandry. There are meeting rooms and wholefood catering in a rural setting.

Publication: Newsletter.

MIDDLE PICCADILLY NEW AGE CENTRE
Holwell
Nr Sherborne, Dorset DT9 5LW
☎ 096 323 468

Middle Piccadilly is a New Age community. They teach and practise various crafts, some of which are explored in groups. Other workshops are concerned with self-exploration, awareness and wholeness. Courses are run throughout the year.

Publication: Newsletter.

THE TEACHERS
18 Garth Road
Bangor, Gwynedd, N. Wales

The Teachers Community is concerned with education. They run training programmes on communal living, choice mathematics and child-rearing. They have a farm, school, computers and a printing press.

Publications: Several books, including two directories covering communities throughout the world.

WARDEN COURT
Presteigne
Powys, Wales
☎ 05444 205

Warden Court is a New Age centre exploring alternative medicine and New Age economics. They have a natural health clinic, crafts shop and market and café. Warden Court holds monthly workshops related to self-help.

NORTH AMERICA

ABODE OF THE MESSAGE
PO Box 396
New Lebanon
NY 12125
☎ 518 794 8090

This is a fairly large community based upon the teachings of Pir Vilayat Inayat Khan who is the head of the Sufi Order of the West. The Abode of the Message is specifically for those who seek a spiritual way of life free from the pressures and problems of the modern world. It is a place where ideals can be lived. The community has its own medical clinic, bakery and stove store. Many community crafts are also prepared. Permanent members average around 100.

Publications: Books by Pir and Hazrat Inayat Khan are available.

ANANDA COOPERATIVE VILLAGE
(c/o David Praver)
14618 Tyler Foote Road
Nevada City, California
☎ 918 292 3494

Ananda is a co-operative spiritual community offering training in practical techniques to bring God into our daily lives. A balance of meditation and outward activity is sought with a goal of even-mindedness and cheerfulness. In a total yogic environment over 200 people experience plain living and high thinking. There are many courses and retreats ranging from meditation to small business management. The village has two schools, a market, dairy and guest facilities.

Publications: 'Spirit and Nature'; the 'Ananda Newspaper'; 'Joy-Song'.

CHINOOK LEARNING COMMUNITY
PO Box 57
Clinton, WA 98236
☎ 206 321 1884

Chinook Learning Community is an educational centre, a covenant community and a vision. Its purpose is to participate in the transformation of all life through attunement to God and by demonstrating the vision of a new age. The programmes are designed to provide a comprehensive vision of the emerging Earth Community and the personal, spiritual, intellectual, cultural, and global issues involved, as well as to train participants in spiritual discipleship and in the translation of vision into practical demonstration and service. A variety of workshops, seminars, retreats, and a year-long intensive Core Studies programme are offered. Other resources include a library, tapes, periodicals and study papers. Chinook holds courses, seminars and workshops on transformational themes.

Publication: 'Warm Wind', journal.

COSANTI FOUNDATION
6433 Doubletree Road
Scottsdale, Arizona 85253
☎ 602 948 6145

Cosanti is an educational foundation sponsoring experiential workshops involved with the design and construction of an experimental new town, Arcosanti, located in the High Mesa country of Arizona.

Publications: Books by Paolo Soleri; Sketchbooks; Fragments; Archeology – 'City in the Image of Man'.

GREVN MADAINN FOUNDATION INC.
Route 2, Box 200
Robbinsville, NC 28771
☎ 704 479 6767

This is a spiritual based community concerned with natural lifestyles, healing and self-improvement. The centre is open to those who wish to help with gardening and building.

Publication: Sporadic newsletter.

GROUP FOR INTEGRATED SERVICE INC.
RT 9
Box 2370
Brooksville
FL 33512
☎ 904 796 1133

The Group is a small community based upon the writings of Alice Bailey. The members promote the study of meditation, healing, esoteric psychology and the creative arts. All these fields which are interrelated may be applied to the 'Science of Service'.

Some of the services of the community include film shows available to other groups, a Montessori Kindergarten and workshops and programmes related to the writings of H. P. Blavatsky, Nicholas Roerich and Alice Bailey.

The community also distributes the music of harpist Joel Andrews.

KARME-CHOLING BUDDHIST MEDITATION CENTRE
Barnet
VT 05821
☎ 802 633 2384

The centre is the major contemplative community for Buddhist meditation under the Kagyu tradition. Founded in 1970 by Chögyam Trungpa the community offers intensive study and meditation and there are a variety of programmes run over weekends, weeks and some over months for those who seek to become instructors of meditation.

The daily programme of the centre is open to the public all year round.

MATAGIRI
Mt Tremper
MY 12457
☎ 914 679 8322

The community, situated on 42 acres of woodland, is based upon the teachings of Sri Aurobindo and the Mother and the application of the principles of Integral Yoga.

Visitors are welcome although accommodation is limited. It should be stated that Matagiri is not a retreat but a working community using the yoga of work.

Publication: Quarterly newsletter containing extracts from the writings of Sri Aurobindo, the Mother and others.

EUROPE

FRATERNITÉ BLANCHE UNIVERSELLE
2 rue de Belvedere de la Ronce
92310 Sevres, France
☎ 1 534 08 85

Welcoming everyone belonging to whatever religion and colour who longs for spiritual unity, the 'Universal White Brotherhood' is based upon a revitalized and enlightened Christianity and Eastern spiritual writings. The intent is to prepare the new mankind of Aquarius and to re-establish the Golden Age on earth.

Publication: Edition Prosveta – a catalogue of publications.

GROUPE DE CHAMARANDE
Chateau de Chamarande
91730 Chamarande, France
☏ 491 2480

This is an educational centre concerned with the new technologies, do-it-yourself, health and harmony. Several courses are open to the public on these subjects and also the exploration of nature.

KOSMOSOPHISCHE GESELLSCHAFT e.V.
Karlstrasse 21 a – Postfach 430 155
D – 7500 Karlsruhe, West Germany
☏ 580 80 755

This group does not represent a specific way of thought or ideology, but rather points out, free from dogmas, universal correlations to achieve a synthesis of scientific-objective and spiritual-subjective experience aimed at a greater understanding among mankind.

REST OF THE WORLD

ANANDA PALLI
Box 3
Severnlea 4352
Queensland, Australia
☏ 835207

This is one of the Ananda Marga farms. Here a life of self-sufficiency is explored within the community framework. The centre also offers spiritual training programmes for those staying at the farm.

AUROVILLE INFORMATION
Auroville
Kottakuppam 605104, India

Auroville wants to be a universal township where men and women of all countries are able to live in peace and progressive harmony, beyond all creeds, all politics, and all nationalities. The purpose of Auroville is to realize human unity.

Auroville, founded in 1968, located in rural South India, is still in the early stage of development. Each one must know if he wants to associate with an old world ready for death, or to work for a new and better world preparing to be born.

Publication: 'Auroville Review', quarterly.

CHOLAMANDAL ARTISTS VILLAGE

Madras-600041, India
☎ 412 892

An artists' village consisting of 37 members promoting Indian art. A unique experiment involving a community lifestyle, a working centre of the arts. There are workshops open to the public to explore all aspects of the arts in India.

Publication: 'Indian Art since the early 1940s'.

CHRIST CONSCIOUSNESS CENTERING

Box 16, Nimbin
2480 Australia
☎ 066 891498

Concerned with resettling unemployed and idealistic people into survival co-operatives. The centre offers other services including legal advice, religious and philosophic study.

Publication: Several pamphlets are available.

HOMELAND CENTRE OF LIGHT

Upper Thora
2492 New South Wales, Australia

This is a New Age community concerned with the anchoring of New Age energies within the patterns of everyday life. The teaching and work of the centre is very much in line with that of Findhorn (see UK listing).

WORLD UNION

Pondicherry 605002
India
☎ 4834

Activities include the publication of books, booklets; seminars and conferences promoting world consciousness, world community, world unity, world government; active collaboration with individuals and movements of similar aims. There are more than 50 World Union Centres in India and a few abroad.

Publications: 'World Union', international monthly journal; newsletter.

6

NETWORKS, ASSOCIATIONS, INFORMATION CENTRES

INTRODUCTION
BY SIR JOHN SINCLAIR

Those who have listened to the Dalai Lama give an address as he travels the world, whether they have attended a meeting in person or seen a filmed recording, will have been struck by the simple core of his theme. Cutting through doctrinal, sectarian or political differences, he always draws attention to the need for that goodwill which lies behind true friendship. The quality of friendliness for which he appeals, is in fact the practical basis of networking. It is easy enough to dismiss as a simplistic sentiment, but a real discipline to practise it successfully.

Time and again it can be observed that people from different persuasions of thought, different areas of work or different services within those areas, who come together to attend events of mutual interest and bother to make friends, turn out to be the communicators through whom successful business accrues and projects flower.

When people suggest a closer liaison between groups of any kind, it is important to remember this. Also, I always mention the example of a successful networking spin-off that came out of World Refugee Year. It was in fact one of the first international 'labelled years' in which a chosen area of need formed a focus of concentrated effort for any groups who cared to be interested. The main objective was of course, to meet the need and clear the refugee problem lingering from world war days. However, just as a seed-thought in meditation can help to integrate consciousness, so, this chosen focus for common effort, simple, practical and vitally necessary to global welfare as it was, provided integrative energy between the very various groups who responded. And it made their co-operation work.

Against the backdrop of any strong world need to which we willingly apply ourselves, petty jealousies based on the size of subscription lists or comparative circulation figures for journals, fade away. The egotistic rivalry of 'leaders' and personalities has little substance on which to build when a responsive heart is open; and the red-tape of ceremony fades in significance when compassion's sun lights the horizon.

Within the unity of such common effort, as we have noted, people make friends. It is these relationships, forged in response to a common vocation, that are the fabric of networks. Like bees, the friends cross-polinate the different 'plantings' and enhance creative enterprise.

For what real meaning have networks of related people, in terms of those movements, groups and services which represent the unfoldment of human consciousness, if they are not in fact part of one overall network created from the broadcast flow of goodwill between outward facing 'stations of light'? Each group unit is autonomous in its own function yet linked in one work; like Schumacher's vision of many individually functioning, specialized work-groups embraced within an overall global vision or subjective pattern.

The concept is so simple that some may wonder why bother to take pen to paper to discuss it, until they make their own effort to test the vision! If you can awaken simultaneously friendship, goodwill and response to real need, then the universal network of light and goodwill is automatically woven. The secret of success lies in the degree of joy with which anyone can make the necessary shifts in identification.

What does that last sentence really mean? Clearly, if people do not want to do something which of its nature is largely dependant on voluntary effort, it is very unlikely to happen. But, if one can find in oneself joy through the action, it may happen with unexpected speed. Happiness in a lifting heart is the great communicator.

And what of identification? It is a question of attitude, of where the sights are focusing. If there is total self-centredness, whether of person or group, networking is unlikely to take place. But when the vision embraces the greater need and the larger area of life, when the flow of energy is radiant and out-going, when social empathy allows a just appreciation of the whole scene and when one can sense the presence of another's 'god', then the network of light and goodwill can become a reality. And so it is 'heart' representing quality and 'eye' representing direction, co-operate in the weaving.

Each era of man's history has reportedly developed its own special yoga or technical means of union with life. These have multiplied and over-lapped, but a further development ever lies ahead. Asana exercises for physical prowess, emotional devotion, mental illumination and other means of self-realization have mounted on each other to form a ladder for the human soul. Prophets now foresee a further potential yoga – a trans-group yoga, the Yoga of Synthesis, the yoga for the whole of life. Networking with the lighted energy of goodwill is one of its first asanas.

UK

COMMONWORK
Bore Place
Bough Beech
Edenbridge, Kent TN8 7AR
☎ 073277 255

Concerned with the care of natural and human resources. Commonwork is situated on a farm and has a conference centre with a programme of workshops concerned with energy and alternative technology.

Publications: Commonwork Information folders; Work Aid; Disarmament tapes.

FUTURE STUDIES CENTRE
15 Kelso Road
Leeds, LJ2 9PR
☎ 0532 459865

The Centre provides a contact point for a network of well over 1000 groups, organizations and individuals in some 40 countries who are concerned about alternative options for the future, such as energy, food, technology, lifestyles, communities, co-operatives, peace, third world, healing, spirituality and environmental concerns. The Centre runs a resource operation and a library.

Publication: 'Future Studies Centre newsletter', bimonthly.

HAWKWOOD COLLEGE
(Bernard J. Nesfield-Cookson, BA, MLitt, Dip. Biol., Principal)
Stroud, Glos. GL6 7QW
☎ 04536 4607

Over and above courses which offer experiences in music, arts and crafts, Hawkwood seeks to foster through a variety of conferences and seminars ways and means to a spiritual foundation for life to counterbalance the materialistic values which dominate most fields of human activity today.

Publication: Six-monthly brochure announcing courses.

LIGHT UPON LIGHTS ARTS COMPANY AND OMEGA ARTS NETWORK

58 St Stephens Gardens
London W2
☎ 01 221 3215

This is a network for artists seeking to create a better world through their art. It publishes an international directory of artists and projects bi-annually, and offers crafts and theatre classes and holistic education for adults and children.

Publication: 'Healing in our Time' (bi-annual journal).

MIND-BODY-SPIRIT

159 George Street
London W1H 5LB
☎ 01 723 7256

The Festival for Mind, Body, Spirit is the largest international New Age festival, held each year in London and elsewhere. Average attendance is 70,000 people. The organizers also run a natural health clinic and information resource centre. Other activities include British regional tours and fayres. They work closely with 'Soluna' magazine.

NADA RECORDS

11 Woodfield Gardens
Leigh-on-Sea, Essex
☎ 0702 72294

Nada Records is involved in the production of meditation/New Age music cassettes and records, and is also a large distributor of spiritual music from all over the world. David Lawrence, the founder, is available to lecture and give demonstrations on music and the spiritual life. Advice is available on music therapy to groups and individuals.

NATIONAL CENTRE FOR ALTERNATIVE TECHNOLOGY

Machynlleth
Powys, Wales
☎ 0654 2400

The Centre is a display centre set up to demonstrate the use of renewable energies. They are a registered charity, independent of government funding, trying to demonstrate the use of sustainable technologies with the minimum of environmental impact.

The Centre is open to the public seven days per week, and has a large mail-order book shop. They also offer residential weekend courses in energy advice on solar, wind, water, design, conservation and organic gardening.

NEW AGE FESTIVAL NETWORK
Rosewood House
Lydbrook
Forest of Dean, Glos. GL17 9SA
☎ 0594 60545

An informal meeting point for organizers of New Age festivals. A calendar of festival events is published twice a year.

NUCLEUS NETWORK AND PLANETARY INITIATIVE
188 Old Street
London EC1
☎ 01 250 1219

The Nucleus Network is the originating point for a number of activities including the 'New Times' magazine (see Magazine section) and the UK Planetary Initiative Co-ordinating team. Nucleus has an information resource of several thousand groups throughout the world.

The Planetary Initiative Co-ordinating Team are working with information networks and resource material and travelling throughout Britain presenting the project and inspiring others to initiate transformation in their local area by setting up groups, hosting panel discussions and discovering the activities of already existing local groups. Planetary Initiative is a response to the impulse to co-operate and widen boundaries, both in personal transformation and within groups, in the spirit of a united vision of one earth, one humanity and one destiny.

TRIANGLES
Suite 54
3 Whitehall Court
London SW1A 2EF
☎ 01 849 4512

Triangles is a meditation technique and service activity for all who believe in the power of thought. The network includes many thousands of people working in over 96 countries. Working in groups of three they help to establish right human relations by creating a worldwide network of light and goodwill.

Publication: A quarterly Triangles Bulletin, published in Dutch, English, French, German, Greek, Italian, Polish, Scandinavian and Spanish editions.

TURNING POINT
Spring Cottage
9 New Road
Ironbridge, Shropshire TF8 7AU
☎ 095 245 2224

Turning Point is an international network of people whose individual concerns range very widely – environment, sex equality, third world, peace and disarmament, community politics, appropriate technology and alternatives in economics, health, education, agriculture, religion, etc., but who share a common feeling that mankind is at a turning point. It sees that old values, old lifestyles and an old system of society are breaking down, and that new ones must be helped to break through. Turning Point does not demand adherence to doctrines, manifestos and resolutions. It enables us, as volunteers, to help and to seek help from one another.

Publications: Turning Point newsletter (twice yearly); 'Redistribution of Work' (Turning Point paper).

UNILIGHT PRODUCTIONS
57 Warescot Road
Brentwood, Essex CM15 9HH

Unilight is a spiritual business, raising finances for the New Age activities of the Lodge of the Star. At this time Unilight Productions is the largest distributor in the world of New Age video tapes covering such fields as health and healing, inner growth, world religions and global concerns. Tapes are available in most formats and many are also produced as 16mm films. Unilight believes in positive media and its commitment to the video market confirms its belief.

Publication: Catalogue of 95 different video titles.

UK CYCLES NETWORK
(Digby Dodd, Chairman)
Sparrow's Barton
Easton
Nr Corsham, Wilts. SN13 9QD
Corsham 713208
☎ 01 353 1884

The widest understanding of the universal laws which influence events and cause changes of behaviour such as peace and wars, social and civil upheaval, health and epidemics, prosperity and depressions, natural disasters etc. is likely to be fundamental to the New Age awareness.

The UK Cycles Network (UCN) is a group of British scientists and many others commonly linked in understanding those natural laws which control all timing, cycles, rhythms, eras and recurring events throughout society and nature in order to help prevent and reduce the effects of these on man and the environment. Contacts, publications, research and seminars are resulting from the Network and its special study groups, which are associated with other groups and individuals internationally.

VOICE OF HEAVEN RECORDING CENTRE/ VOICE OF HEAVEN RECORDS

46 Charles Street
Berkhamsted, Herts
☎ 04427 6581

VHRC exists to promote music which carries the spirit of the New Age. They are involved in the organization of concerts, festivals, recording and producing music, manufacture, distribution and music promotion.

THE WESSEX RESEARCH GROUP NETWORK

Nigel Blair
Beech Cottage
79 Acreman Street
Sherborne, Dorset DT9 3PH
☎ 093 581 2353

The Wessex Research Group is a co-ordinating network and focus for groups and individuals concerned with new areas of research and experience. They are particularly interested in spiritual, cultural, artistic, historical, ecological and scientific fields. The Group holds events and lectures throughout historic Wessex in the hope of promoting awareness of the area's unique mystical and cultural heritage. Many prominent speakers take part in their programmes.

Publication: Regular lecture and event programme.

WORLD COUNCIL OF UNITY AND SERVICE

1 St Georges Square
Lytham St Annes, Lancs
☎ 0253 721504

A humanitarian organization concerned with the spiritual advancement of man and the development of world peace – world economic reforms – political unity and stability among all nations of the world.

Publication: 'C-O-M-P-O-S-I-T-E'.

NORTH AMERICA

ARCANA WORKSHOPS
PO Box 5105
Beverly Hills, Ca. 90210-0105

Arcana is a training centre for volunteer community servers. All staff members are volunteers and the centre's work is financed entirely by volunteer donations.

A triple programme is offered: progressively advanced *meditation training* appropriate for today's living, which raises, refines, expands, and inspires the individual's consciousness; systematic *study* of the grades of matter, types of energy, and levels of consciousness that make up the field of human evolution; group experience that develops human relations skills in a co-operative atmosphere.

Publication: 'Thoughtline', monthly.

AMERICAN ASSOCIATION FOR TRANSPERSONAL PSYCHOLOGY
345 California Avenue, Suite 1
Palo Alto, Ca. 94306
☎ 415 327 2066

The Association conducts an annual conference held each summer as well as special interest conferences. Members receive a newsletter published quarterly and related information on other events. Membership is open to all those interested in transpersonal psychology and transpersonal values.

Publication: 'Association for Transpersonal Psychology' newsletter.

ASSOCIATION FOR HUMANISTIC PSYCHOLOGY
325 Ninth Street
San Francisco, Ca 94103
☎ 415 626 2375

AHP exists to link, for support and stimulation, people who have a humanistic vision of the person and are applying these principles; to foster research and education which broadens the base of human inquiry to honour experiential and subjective data; to foster and support the realization of human potential, self-determination, and self-actualization for all persons.

Publications: AHP Newsletter; 'Journal of Humanistic Psychology'; 'AHP Resource Directory'.

THE BOSTON VISIONARY CELL

36 Bromfield Street, Room 200
Boston, Mass. 02108
☎ 617 482 9044

The Boston Visionary Cell is primarily an association of Neo-Platonic artists and others from disciplines which act as supporters and consultants, for the purpose of fostering visionary art, considered as an eternal genre – otherwise known as cosmic, cosmological, magical, mystical, or occult art – in the Boston and New England area.

Publication: Brochure.

CONSCIOUSNESS SYNTHESIS CLEARINGHOUSE (CONSYNC)

523 Camino de Encanto
Redondo Beach, Ca 90277
☎ 213 375 8086

CONSYNC is a Network Dialogue catalyst committed to facilitating the networking process as a tool for transformation via workshops, writing, educational and consulting services. CONSYNC works with groups and individuals to explore possibilities for linking and pooling resources.

Publication: 'Idealogue'.

INTERNATIONAL SOCIETY OF FRIENDSHIP AND GOOD WILL

PO Box 871
Shelby, North Carolina 28150
☎ 704 487 5873

The main objective of this Society is to 'encourage and foster the advancement of international understanding, friendship, good will, and peace through a world fellowship of business and professional men and women'; and 'to promote international friendship week in the USA,

Canada, and throughout the world'. They offer instruction in Esperanto, in classes and through home-study.

INTERNATIONAL TEILHARD FOUNDATION

2290 Emerald Road
Boulder, Colorado 80302
☎ 303 443 3647

A global network which offers a quarterly newsletter, an annual conference, an annual prize, international round tables, access to resources, speakers' bureau and writers' bank, and hundreds of local activities. The ITF is a world-wide network of people actively engaged in developing a global culture. Its members are from every walk of life, every racial, religious, economic and social group on every continent. The ITF engages in a variety of research, educational, communications and action projects, some of which are described above.

Publication: 'Noosphere'.

LINKAGE INC.

4221 W. Yucca Street
Phoenix, Az. 85029
☎ 602 938 4849

Linkage is a network for people and organizations involved in social transformation, especially within the context of community. Members wishing to act as resources send in an information sheet which is circulated throughout the network, primarily North American, with some overseas members.

Publication: Linkage Information Packet.

MOVEMENT FOR A NEW SOCIETY

4722 Baltimore Avenue
Philadelphia 19143
☎ 215 724 1464

The Movement for a New Society is a nationwide network of small groups working for basic social change. Non-violent action, just lifestyles and democratic process are essential to their efforts. Their approach is to look carefully at where they are now; create a vision of a better world; and then to work out ways for getting from the present situation to that kind of society. Since important changes don't happen overnight, they are expecting to struggle non-violently for many years, developing alternatives to the existing society which are rooted in our own evolving values; and building a movement that will work for those alternatives. A literature list is available on request.

NEW ALCHEMY INSTITUTE
237 Hatchville Road
East Falmouth, MA 02536

The Institute seeks to develop ecological approaches to food, energy, shelter and community design, emphasizing a minimal reliance on fossil fuels and on a scale accessible to families and small enterprises. Guided tours are available around the New Alchemy Institute.

Publications: 'The New Alchemy Quarterly'; 'The Journal of the New Alchemists'.

PLANETARY CITIZENS
777 United Nations Plaza
New York, NY 10017
☎ 212 10017

The concept and feeling of global oneness – of mutual brotherhood and interdependence among all human inhabitants of the earth – is not limited to the astronauts. Almost spontaneously, the need was recognized by concerned people in many countries: the human family must find a way to work together if human life on earth is to be preserved and improved. Such co-operation is intended in the originating spirit of the United Nations. There, in May 1970, the concept of planetary unity emerged in tangible form at the Conference on Human Survival. Hosted by U Thant and Chaired by Lester Pearson of Canada, participants in this important conference later worked with Norman Cousins, U Thant and Donald Keys in developing an organization of international scope: Planetary Citizens. The programme was officially launched in May 1972, at a press conference led by U Thant.

The response was immediate. The registration programme – first begun as a pilot programme in the USA and Canada – brought response from people in more than fifty countries. To date, over 200,000 individuals have affirmed their global citizenship by endorsing the Pledge and registering as Planetary Citizens.

Today, Planetary Citizenship is developing rapidly on an international scale. For those actively seeking for ways to help, Planetary Citizens is functioning as a major resource in the world community. It is a place to learn, to join energies with others, to help groups and individuals alike get started with their projects. There is nothing else quite like it in human history. We are crossing a threshold in human development.

Publications: 'One Family' newsletter; 'Planet Earth' magazine.

THE ROUNDTABLE OF THE LIGHT CENTERS
1801 SW 82 Place
Miami, Florida 33155
☎ 305 264 4118

The Roundtable of the Light Centers is a New Age association whose main purpose is to increase co-operation and manifest harmony among all spiritual, religious, psychic, scientific and philosophical individuals and groups in the South Florida area. They also strive to serve their communities as an educational, cultural and social forum. Their goal is to remove the barriers that separate us as individuals and groups, so that all may be enriched by the pooling of collective energies and resources for the benefits of man.

Monthly meetings produce attendance up to an average of 250 people, at which lectures, demonstrations, panel discussions and films are presented. Their format has great diversity in subject-matter which includes healing, hypnosis, UFOs, astrology, dreams, mediumship, yoga, tarot, parapsychology, tai-chi, radiesthesia, meditation, pyramids, reincarnation, etc. They have no dogma but strive to expose members to a diversity of thought, philosophy and theory, so that they can choose whatever approach or belief suits them. There is a Central Information Bureau which provides information about community events. Healers Anonymous – an absent healing 'broadcast' by anonymous healers – goes out six times a day.

Publications: 'The Beacon', monthly eight-page newsletter describing community activities and forthcoming events; Roundtable Directory – a reference guide listing individuals and groups, their speciality and phone numbers, etc.

SPIRITUAL ADVISORY COUNCIL, INC.
New Age Community Centre
2500 E. Curry Ford Road
Orlando, Fl. 32806
☎ 305 898 2500

Educational and religious organization, church and association of churches to extend opportunities for insights into prayer, psychic and spiritual development, and healing. Ministers are ordained into healing service.

Publication: Monthly newsletter to members.

TRANET

PO Box 567
Rangeley, Maine 04970
☎ 207 864 2252

Tranet is a decentralized, trans-national network of appropriate and alternative technology practitioners. The network's function is to facilitate the exchange of ideas and information between the practitioners.

Publication: Tranet quarterly newsletter-directory.

UNITY IN DIVERSITY COUNCIL

c/o World Trade Center
350 S. Figueroa Street, Suite 370
Los Angeles, Ca. 90071
☎ 213 626 2062

A world-wide co-ordinating body of organizations and individuals who foster unity-in-diversity amongst all peoples. The Council has a membership of about 200 groups and these are encouraged to co-operate and come together on joint projects. The Council holds a yearly festival which stresses unity-in-diversity.

Publications: Spectrum magazine; Directory for a New World (published each year).

WORLD FUTURE SOCIETY

4916 54 Elmo Avenue
Bethesda, Maryland 20814
☎ 301 656 8274

The Society is an association of people interested in future social and technological developments. It is chartered as a non-profit scientific and educational organization in Washington, DC, and is recognized as tax-exempt by the US Internal Revenue Service. The World Future Society is independent, non-political and non-ideological.

The purpose of the WFS is to serve as unbiased forum and clearing-house for scientific and scholarly forecasts, investigations and intellectual explorations of the future. The Society's objectives, as stated in its charter, are as follows:

1 To contribute to a reasoned awareness of the future and the importance of its study, without advocating particular ideologies or engaging in political activities.

2 To advance responsible and serious investigation of the future.

3 To promote the development and improvement of methodologies for the study of the future.

4 To increase public understanding of future-oriented activities and studies.

5 To facilitate communication and co-operation among organizations and individuals interested in studying or planning for the future.

Membership is open to anyone seriously interested in the future. Since its founding in 1966, the Society has grown to more than 40,000 members in over 80 countries. Most members are residents of the USA, with growing numbers in Canada, Europe, Japan, and other countries. Members include many of the world's most distinguished scientists, scholars, business leaders and government officials.

Publication: 'The Futurist'.

EUROPE

INTERNATIONAL PEACE INFORMATION SERVICE
Kerkstraat 150
2000 Antwerpen
Belgium
☎ 031/35 02 72

The service is primarily concerned with peace research and its relationship with the peace movement. The service presents information which is available to everyone as a result of its vital networking of groups concerned with action and research for peace.

OMKRESTON
Nowfullsgaten 53
11345 Stockholm
Sweden

The network was formed to promote all forms of spiritual awareness within Swedish society and actively seeks to bring together like-minded people. Through their work there has been an increased demand for New Age speakers and a growing interest has been shown from Swedish radio and TV in New Age matters.

THE REST OF THE WORLD

ARKEN LEARNING EXCHANGE
c/o Turntable Falls Community
PO Nimbin 2480, Australia

This is an information service for New Age activities in Australia and can provide news on projects, groups and centres operating within the broad spectrum of the counter culture.

DOWN TO EARTH MOVEMENT
427 Cleveland Street
Surrey Hills
New South Wales, Australia
☎ 696 237

The movement has contact and links with many community projects in Australia and can provide information on most alternative lifestyles via its information centre. This is certainly the contact point for Australian self-sufficient/ecological communes.

THE INDO-AMERICAN SOCIETY
Kitab Mahal
5 Raveline Street
Fort, Bombay 400 001, India
☎ 26 48 82–83

The Indo-American Society's aims and objects are: the dissemination of knowledge and education and the promotion of understanding between the people of India and the people of the United States of America; the true appreciation of the ways of life, cultures and languages of the peoples of these countries; the promotion of enduring goodwill, friendship and co-operation in all spheres of life, thought and activity between the people of these countries.

NEW AWARENESS CENTRE
12 Thomas Street
Chatswood
New South Wales, Australia 2067
☎ 02 4124725

The New Awareness Centre maintains a bookshop on all New Age subjects and also operates a Resource and Information Centre. It helps to organize tours, festivals and symposiums in Australia and is therefore a very useful contact point for much New Age activity.

Publication: 'Southern Crossings' (free).

7

MAGAZINES
AND JOURNALS

UK

CENTRE PUBLICATIONS
11 Rowacres
Bath, BA2 2LH
☎ 0225 26327

Centre Publications are UK and European distributors of California's 'Yoga Journal' and a range of holistic and yoga books. The 'Yoga Journal' is a leading USA publication focusing on holistic lifestyles.

CREATIVE MIND
Lark Lane Community Centre
80 Lark Lane
Liverpool L17
☎ 051 727 6917

Creative Mind is a humanistic and person-centred organization concerned with community affairs. They have a centre for the promotion of personal growth and awareness and also operate an information service, run courses and produce a 'Journal of Alternatives'. Creative Mind is sympathetic to environmental matters, education, psychological health and new approaches to living together.

Publication: 'Creative Mind', national quarterly.

FORESIGHT

29 Beaufort Avenue
Hodge Hill, Birmingham B34 6AD
☎ 021 783 0587

Bi-monthly magazine concerned about the world and its problems on all levels, physical, mental, psychic and spiritual. It encourages the spiritual awareness and evolution of humanity in the true spirit of the New Age. It also deals with such subjects as UFOs, psychic phenomena, spiritualism, mysticism, the occult, etc.

FOURTH WORLD NEWS

24 Abercorn Place
London NW8
☎ 01 286 4366

A journal produced for small nations and small communities and the human spirit. Contains political and economic analysis.

HUMAN POTENTIAL RESOURCES

35 Station Road
London NW4
☎ 01 202 4941

Human Potential Resources is a directory and information service covering that broad spectrum of activities that is called the human potential movement. The magazine is intended as a service to those who are searching for new directions to take in their personal development and growth.

INTERCHANGE

Holne Cross Cottage
Ashburton, Devon

A quarterly journal devoted to human evolution on earth, associated with the Teilhard Centre, promoting the vision of hope and belief in the future of Teilhard de Chardin. It is also a personal sharing-space for people who dream, for people who know that 'all this could be different', and that the earth can be a place in which we can strive to realize our dreams, and create the truly 'real' among ourselves.

THE NEW HUMANITY JOURNAL
51a York Mansions
Prince of Wales Drive
London SW11
☎ 01 622 4013

The world's first politico-spiritual journal for the free and independent thinker. Current circulation is approximately 14,000. The journal has a worldwide readership with links with many groups. The editor, Johann Quanier, is available to lecture on the politico-spiritual arena.

NEW TIMES
188 Old Street
London EC1
☎ 01 250 1219

The journal informs people about ways of taking positive steps to improve their lives and their environment. 'New Times' gives detailed information about New Age events, projects and developments with articles on important themes. The journal provides a platform for groups and individuals to synthesize by using the magazine as a platform. The emphasis is on positivity rather than negativity.

OPEN CENTRE NEWSLETTER
Avils Farm
Lower Stanton
Chippenham, Wilts
☎ 0249 720202

This bi-annual newsletter links centres, groups, private houses and friends who share the desire to be open to the truth through meditation, movement, healing and interfaith work. The journal includes articles and a useful list of addresses. Circulation is 2,500.

PEACE TAX CAMPAIGN
26 Thurlow Road
Leicester LE2 1YE
☎ 0533 702687

To secure legislation which will enable taxpayers to divert a proportion of their income tax away from so-called defence to positive peace-making projects. Circulation is 4,500 and rising steadily.

QUEST

(Marian Green, editor)
BCM – SCL Quest
London WC1N 3XX

Quest quarterly journal has been published regularly since March 1970. It covers all practical and philosophical aspects of ritual, divination, natural magic, witchcraft and allied subjects. Teaching on these subjects is offered by post and at residential weekend courses. An annual conference is held each March.

RESURGENCE

(Satish Kumar, editor)
Ford House
Hartland
Bideford, Devon

'Resurgence' is an established magazine dealing with peace, decentralist thinking, small nations and small communities. It contains articles from many of today's most prominent thinkers. Circulation is approximately 4,000.

REVELATION

8 Victoria Court
Victoria Road
New Brighton
Wirral, Merseyside L45 9LD

Revelation is a journal for the study of the ageless wisdom and New Age teachings.

SCIENCE OF THOUGHT REVIEW

Bosham House
Chichester
P018 8PJ

This is a monthly magazine devoted to the teaching of Applied Right Thinking. Each issue contains a wealth of material covering the spiritual field. The journal is available for a minimum yearly subscription of only 25p. Its editor is Clare Cameron who has maintained this high service for many years.

SEMPERVIVUM MAGAZINE

c/o Salisbury Centre
2 Salisbury Road
Edinburgh EH16 5AB
☎ 031 667 5438

A Scottish guide to meditation, yoga, groupwork, counselling, healing
and other approaches to self-fulfilment, published quarterly.

SKILL PUBLICATIONS

100 Waterloo Road
Blackpool, Lancs FY4 1AW
☎ 0253 403548

Responsible for 'Skill Bulletin' newsletter and provides information on
health and fitness, physical therapies, etc.

SOLACE MAGAZINE

15 Chesham Road
Amersham, Bucks. HP6 5JQ
☎ 02403 6846

'Solace' is published by the Universal Peace Mission which is non-sectarian and whose aims are to help solve problems which create chaos and
division in life. Its contents therefore cover every aspect of life, whether
social, cultural, political, economic or spiritual. Solace guides, inspires
and clarifies wherever there is confusion in people's minds about life in
general, and promotes ideas which are wholly designed to carry mankind
into a new age of peace, love and unity.

SPHERE

c/o 33B Castlegate
Jedburgh, Roxburghshire

'Sphere' is aimed at the uncommitted public such as those who go to yoga
classes, but usually hold aloof from 'New Age' thinking or activities. It
aims at a holistic approach to life and offers articles on many apparently
unrelated topics. A key feature is the use of vignettes, poetry and dec-
orative advertisements.

THE VEGETARIAN

Parkdale, Dunham Road
Altringcham, Cheshire
☎ 061 928 0793

A bi-monthly journal produced by the Vegetarian Society concerned with nutrition and health. A well-produced magazine promoting vegetarianism.

NORTH AMERICA

THE CHURCHMAN
1074 23rd Avenue North
St Petersburg, Fla. 33704
☎ 813 894 0097

'The Churchman' is a Humanist-oriented journal, founded in 1804. It has a positive peace editorial policy; its articles are peace-oriented.

COEVOLUTION QUARTERLY
PO Box 428
Sausalito, California 94966
☎ 415 332 1716

'Coevolution Quarterly' publishes conceptual news, reviews of useful tools and books and interesting articles on topics not covered by other journals. It is also responsible for the 'Whole Earth Catalogue'.

CONNEXIONS
427 Bloor Street West
Toronto, Ontario M5S 1X7, Canada
☎ 416 960 3903

'Connexions' is a quarterly journal which attempts to link Canadians who are involved in the struggle for justice. Recent issues have focused on children, gays and lesbians, militarism and urban core development.

DROMENON JOURNAL
GPO Box 2244
New York, NY 10116
☎ 212 675 3486

Bi-annual journal (thematic) offering transformational information in many areas of 'New Age', especially consciousness research, education, therapy, economics as mythic metaphor. Scholarly in tone yet highly visual and readable.

EAST WEST JOURNAL
17 Station Street
Brookline, MA 02146
☎ 617 232 1000

For over ten years, EWJ has been in the vanguard of the holistic health and natural foods movement. The journal provides practical tools for improving its readers' lives and ideas for re-establishing the health and well-being of their family, friends and community.

FREE SPIRIT
PO Box 279
Riverdale, New York 10471
☎ 212 543 5536

This is a free newspaper directory for the New York area concerning itself with alternative and holistic health services and practitioners, spiritual groups and New Age activities. Contains a wealth of material. 100,000 copies distributed three times a year.

GOLDEN RAYS
PO Box 1088
Glendale, Arizona 85311

A journal providing news of events and groups around the USA. A useful service tool with an excellent news coverage.

THE L.A. LIGHT DIRECTORY
4026 Beverly Boulevard
Los Angeles, California 90004
☎ 213 739 0190

Another free newspaper directory covering the Los Angeles area. A comprehensive resource publication with over 250 regular group listings. Published quarterly with a 40,000 circulation.

LAUGHING MAN MAGAZINE
PO Box 3680
Clearlake, CA. 95422
☎ 707 994 8281

The 'Laughing Man Magazine' considers the truth of our existence, and the truth of the entire 'Great Tradition' of religious, spiritual and philosophical persuasions that we have inherited in this era.

THE MOVEMENT NEWSPAPER
PO Box 19458
Los Angeles, Ca 90019
☎ 213 737 1134

A monthly publication reporting the news of the New Age. Columns include teachers, health, astrology and practical ways to lift your spirits on your inner and outer journey.

NEW AGE MAGAZINE
Box 1200
Allston, MA 02134
☎ 617 254 5400

'New Age Magazine' is a monthly publication offering positive and uplifting ideas in a very practical, down-to-earth way. It presents news and how-to articles about breakthroughs in the fields of holistic health, alternative energy, education, politics, the arts, human potential and self-development. By enhancing the individual's sense of empowerment, it offers a fresh and 'up' perspective on the challenges facing the world.

NEW TEXAS
PO Box 12165
Austin, Texas 78711
☎ 512 476 3131

'New Texas' has resources for changing times, in fields as diverse as holistic health, religion, alternative energy and business services. A bimonthly tabloid format newspaper, free locally.

PARABOLA MAGAZINE
150 Fifth Avenue
New York, NY 10011
☎ 212 924 0004

It is through myth that human beings have always sought to understand themselves, to ponder the deepest human mysteries and to express universal values. 'Parabola', the magazine dedicated to myth and tradition, seeks to open ways into the vital inner dimension – the meeting place between the visible and the invisible, the inner and the outer, the above and the below – and to thereby enrich the experience of our daily life. 'Parabola', a quarterly that explores the worlds of ancient and living traditions in all cultures, invites you to join them in their quest for

meaning where myth is not the imagined world without, but the real world within.
Circulation: 40,000.

PATHWAYS/YES EDUCATION SOCIETY
1033 31st Street, NW
Washington DC 20007
☎ 202 338 7675

Pathways is a 64-page quarterly directory of personal and social transformation, with a circulation of 40,000.

PSYCHOSYNTHESIS PRESS
PO Box 18559
Irvine, Cal. 92713
☎ 714 644 5347

Psychosynthesis Press publishes the 'Psychosynthesis Digest', a professional digest for psychotherapists, educators, ministers and counsellors.

RESOURCES
4422 Alabama Street
San Diego, CA 92116
☎ 714 296 5991

'Resources' is a journal of positive lifestyles and a guide to quality goods and services, providing a showcase for businesses and services which assist us in achieving and maintaining well-being. The journal focuses on commentaries on issues of health, harmony, innovation, prosperity and community.

SCIENCE OF MIND MAGAZINE
PO Box 75127
Los Angeles, Ca 91020
☎ 213 388 2181

The Science of Mind is a spiritual philosophy for the New Age. It is a correlation of laws of science, opinions of philosophy, and revelations of religion, applied to human needs and the aspirations of man. The journal explores these areas without dogma and outdated concepts.

THE UNIVERSAL LISTENING POST
Box 68
Tulip Lane
Sarahsville, Ohio 43779
☎ 614 732 2747

'Open Word', a 4–8 page newsletter published six times a year, concerned with the development of Oneness in Consciousness.

WHOLE LIFE TIMES
132 Adams Street
Newton, Mass 02158
☎ 617 964 7600

'Whole Life Times' is a 'natural lifestyle' publication covering many holistic subjects, such as the environment, natural food, healthy living, and peace.

EUROPE

COEVOLUTION
75 rue Pernety
Paris 75014, France
BP43 75661 Paris Cedex 14, France
☎ 1 543 1017

French quarterly magazine devoted to all aspects of the New Age: whole systems thinking, ecology, appropriate technology, human rights, education, consciousness expansion, New Age politics, etc. Links different ways of knowledge and expression, sciences, philosophy, art, etc.

NEXUS Magazine
Drottninggatan 102
S-111 60 Stockholm, Sweden
☎ 08 11 17 81

Magazine concerned with the human potential movement, the new age and humanistic psychology.

REST OF THE WORLD

ODYSSEY Magazine

PO Box 1709
Cape Town 8000, South Africa
☎ 021 46 5594

'Odyssey' provides a forum for New Age ideas, activities and reports and interviews. All areas are covered through contact with readers. 'Odyssey' is an extremely well-produced journal with excellent articles and reports.

MUSHROOM

PO Box 6098
Dunedin North
New Zealand

This is a bi-monthly alternative periodical and is a national networking instrument extensively read in New Zealand.

THE SIKH REVIEW

Room No. 116
Karnani Mansion
25 Park Street
Calcutta 700016, India
☎ 003 24 9656

The journal works towards the establishment of a better understanding amongst all peoples. It has important features on Sikh religion and Punjabi culture.

ZIRIUS

PO Box 563
Frankston
Victoria, 3199, Australia

'Zirius' is a major networking operation for Australia, bringing together groups and projects. It is also an excellent information source and an ideal contact point for news and group information in Australia.

CONCLUSION
THE NEW PILGRIMAGE
BY SIR GEORGE TREVELYAN

Pilgrimage – a new concept of modern pilgrimage seems to be emerging and it may prove to be of deep significance for the spiritual awakening in our time. In medieval centuries hundreds of thousands of pilgrims streamed between the holy centres and shrines. What was the motive force for this extraordinary phenomenon? Across all European frontiers they came, walking or riding, like Chaucer's Canterbury pilgrims, along established routes to reach a centre made sacred by the relics of some saint. Thus the hope was to get healing of bodily ills and salvation of soul by actually going to the holy spot to pray and give alms to the monastery or cathedral. In the Age of Faith many were still actively aware of the guardian beings, the angelic presences of the shrine. To them the pilgrims came in mood of worship and of wonder.

We may imagine a holy man settling as a hermit in his hut, built on a spot in which he found he could make the breakthrough in consciousness to the higher worlds. After his death a shrine or chapel is built and since healing power appears to be active, this may later become church or cathedral, guarding the holy relics which are believed to have supernatural power. When the pilgrim stream grew, it brought wealth to the monastery or minster. It became the goal of penitent Christians to make a pilgrimage for salvation of their souls. Often such a journey would have been undertaken as a penance for wrong-doing. On the recognized routes, stages of the journey are marked by hostelries and churches. Thus the great pilgrim route to Compostella has on it a wonderful series of Romanesque churches with carvings which must have filled the pilgrims with wonder and delight. The serving and exploiting of the pilgrims became a source of profit for many, just as the tourist industry has grown up in our time. Canterbury and Chartres, Glastonbury and Rosslyn Chapel, Bourges and Vezeley, Durham and Lindisfarne, Mont St Michel and St Michaels Mount, Westminster and Ely – Europe is covered with a network of pilgrim routes. The steps to Becket's shrine in Canterbury are worn hollow by the knees of the innumerable pilgrims who had achieved their goal. And, of course, the ultimate pilgrimage was to the Holy Land, and here the impulse grew into the Crusades.

With the change in consciousness marked by the Renaissance, the impulse to pilgrimage fades. In our time once again innumerable people stream through the churches. So many millions come to Westminster Abbey and Chartres that it becomes a problem how to control and channel the flow. But what really on a deeper level is moving them all? Tourism has debased pilgrimage in an age which is largely agnostic and on the quest for pleasure and diversion. This is a picture of our state of consciousness. But that consciousness is undergoing the most notable change which is truly epoch-making in its significance.

The 'Holistic World-View' is emerging in our generation, a veritable reversal of the materialistic, mechanistic and reductionist picture of the universe discovered by our grandfathers. The materialistic interpretation of life is dissolving to give place to a revival of the ancient wisdom, which grasped that the universe is an affair of mind, a vast harmonious continuance of thought poured out from the mind of the creator. The whole is holy. It is something hugely more than the mere sum of its parts. It is alive – we must stretch our minds to conceive and experience a vast ocean of life and thought, of love and will, existing on an ethereal plane beyond time and filling all space. From this realm of creative idea the physical world of matter and nature is expressed – pressed forth into form. Thus the earth is seen as a living organism with its own breathing and bloodstream, its glands and sensitivity and its own intelligence. Mankind, so far from being an accident in natural selection to whom nature is wholly indifferent, is seen as integrally part of nature, the point where nature becomes self-conscious. Therefore he is clearly the steward of the planet. Indeed the human race is seen as one of the great experiments of God in evolving a being 'a little lower than the angels but crowned with glory and honour', who can learn to carry the divine gift of free will and become in due time a co-creator with God. Thus earth appears as the training ground for the 10th hierarchy. In Blake's words:

> We are set on Earth a little space
> That we may learn to bear the beams of love.

The hermetic wisdom recognized the basic law of correspondences. As above so below. Microcosm reflects macrocosm. The human body is thus the microcosm, reflecting the greater organism, as every fragment in a broken holographic plate shows the entire picture.

You don't get a living organism floating around in a dead mechanism. Thus the solar system is seen as a greater organism, the series of planets corresponding to the endocrine glands in our bodies. These glands relate to the chakras or psychic centres through which living energies flow from the cosmos into the body.

Now our imagination grapples with the discoveries about ley-lines and centres of light and magnetic power in the earth. Dowsers can now research into the flow of earth energies. Alfred Watkins, first discoverer of ley lines, thought them to be trackways and had no adequate explanation of their purpose. Now we recognize that they can represent the lines of the living earth energies linking centres of power. Grace Cooke, as clairvoyant and sensitive, in her book 'The Light in Britain', describes how she saw Avebury and Stonehenge as temples in which, by ancient ritual, spiritual light was stored, to flow in healing along the lines marked by standing stones. Truly they compared to our electrical generating stations from which the power is carried to remote parts by the lines of pylons.

We grasp now the concept of a network of light centres covering the country like a grid. As Watkins showed and modern dowsing reveals, the Christian churches are constantly built on crossing points of ley lines or other focal points of power. It would be fascinating to make a map of Britain showing the ancient sites and the Druidical centres placed upon them. Then imagine this overlaid with a perspex sheet with all Christian churches, cathedrals and monasteries marked on it, and see how often they overlay the pagan centres. Then make another sheet of New Age centres and we should see how frequently the centres of the alternative lifestyle, springing up all over the country, actually fall on the points of light and power. Those who are dedicating their lives to New Age work seem frequently to be led by invisible guidance to settle on significant spots where the energy flows.

CONCLUSION

Indications have been given from the high sources that we are called on to do all we can to strengthen this grid of light. We all foresee the coming of moments of great tension in the Armageddon battle between the forces of darkness (the Beast of the Apocalypse) and the heavenly powers of the Archangel Michael. The supreme hope which can fire all our hearts with courage, is that in the moment of ultimate tension there may be an inflooding of the power of the Living Christ. Light could be poured through human souls and bodies. Those who reject it will be battered and overwhelmed by it. Those who can open the heart and attune to the angelic energies will be lifted with strength and joy. It is something of a science fiction picture – but why not? The alternative is a nuclear holocaust which, to say the least, is sensational!

The implication is that the grid of light centres, power points and holy mountains may be used for flooding spiritual light with transforming power through the whole country. If nature is to receive this inflow of energy, raising the very frequency rate within all matter, then obviously the chief channel of inflow will be that point in nature which has become self-conscious, namely man. The human heart can receive the inflow of divine power. Earth energies may be activated in a cleansing operation to de-pollute the planet.

Now we see the meaning of the New Pilgrimage. Since mankind has been given free will, it is certain that the heaven world will not interfere and take over to the detriment of human freedom. Disasters still leave us free, and may be necessary if we do not wake up and change our evil ways. But if a sufficient number of human beings can see what is happening and consciously attune to the forces of the Living Christ and His Regent Michael, then the great Operation Redemption can fulfil its purpose.

We are called on now to devise ways of linking and activating the dormant light centres, each of which has its angelic guardians. Let us go not merely as tourists, but as pilgrims, recognizing a conscious task of preparing the way for the inflooding of the light when the great moment comes. Whenever we enter a shrine, church or holy place, we should greet its guardian and pray for the incoming of the healing light. Simple ritual of perambulation, poetry, candlelight, dance and music may be devised where appropriate (respecting the feelings and convenience of other tourists). New rituals can validly be invented. They will often be given to us, born in our minds with a strange certainty, since they come from our higher self or the angels who speak with the still small voice within our own thinking. As we leave the place we should always give thanks and blessings to the guardian. As we travel the countryside we should make our journey into a conscious pilgrim-age. We are integrally part of nature and the being of the earth, and when we rejoice in the beauty of scenery, we *are* nature herself coming awake. All life becomes poetry and the earth herself is not quite the same after we have journeyed over her in this pilgrim mood. We are part of the Awakening.

Thus we are rediscovering the holy mountains and the landscape temples. By temple we mean a structure which enables a divine being to operate in the heavier density of the earth plane. Thus the Greek temple was a point where Apollo or Athena could touch down without being contaminated by the coarseness of matter. The Egyptian temple has clearly the same pattern of chakras as is found in the human body, and the same is true in the Gothic cathedral. Microcosm and macrocosm again. We see that the human body with its psychic centres is truly a temple into which the divine spark of the immortal, imperishable ego can descend to operate with creative will on earth.

So we begin to discover and explore the landscape temples, etheric structures which manifest the same pattern of base centres, solar plexus, heart, throat, brow and crown centres. These are not man-made structures, but antedate man, as part of the living organism of the earth. They may be great or small. Thus Britain is a heart centre of the earth, but London is a heart centre of Britain. And many landscape temples may be a few miles long, lying along a ley line. They are visible to clairvoyant sensitivity which can see the inflow of divine angelic light.

Here is a new field of exploration. It really means learning to work with the energies of the earth and it may have an important part to play in the coming changes. Pilgrimage here takes on a new and vital function. As we in our groups undertake pilgrimages with dedicated intent, we shall be establishing and encouraging the flow of healing light and power, and linking up the grid of light centres, that it may be strong to hold the flow of the Christ power when it comes. Sensitives can see the flow of energy in a cathedral. There are apparently definite lines of flow, which can be detected by dowsers. If these can be consciously channelled, it would release spiritual power. Already we see signs of attempts to turn the stream of tourists into something of pilgrimage. Think what it would mean if all the thousands who stream through Mont St Michel had taken on the conscious task. The breathtaking loveliness and wonder of Chartres, which often moves to tears, comes very close to a real pilgrim impulse. It only needs a little change of emphasis to illumine the enthusiasm for art with a sense of the living and present reality of the angelic being portrayed in stained glass and sculpture. The awakening of the spiritual world-view gives us this necessary vision and we may go to the great works of ancient art knowing that they speak direct to the soul of the reality of higher worlds and the coming of the Christ impulse anew in our time.

In our cathedrals we could easily invite people to feel themselves as pilgrims and follow the ancient routes within the building used by the pilgrims of medieval days. Already the attempt is being made to encourage meditation as we move around.

Consider how favourable is the climate of our time for a revival of Pilgrimage. There has been a wonderful impetus to art and architectural history given since the war, through the lead of the great art historians and the publication of beautiful books with modern photography. This is heightened by the development of tourist facilities and the delight of 'going places'. When these two factors link with the awakening vision of the spiritual nature of man and the universe, then 'Pilgrimage' in a real and true sense must begin again.

This spiritual world-view calls for interpretation. In each of the great arts we discover that the angelic wisdom, expressing the great truth of man's spiritual nature, has in its own symbolism told the story of his descent from the heavenly spheres into the struggles of earth life. In Blake's phrase he has passed from innocence through experience to imagination. All the arts will be re-interpreted and a new creative inspiration will come as men and women awaken to spiritual vision. And as we open to fourth dimensional awareness, more and more people will begin to see the angelic beings in the holy centres. Already those in whom these faculties are awake begin to take guided tours to Greece, and Egypt, the Holy Land and the great cathedrals. The 'esoteric' tour is becoming a function with wonderful opportunities. It is a true aspect of the revival of Pilgrimage.

But more than this, we enter the last two decades of the twentieth century and stand on the threshold of the Aquarian Age, when energies for the cleansing of the planet are flooding through the earth. It is a dramatic time, an apocalyptic time. We all know that if mankind continues in his folly, greed and ignorance, the living earth of which he is the errant steward, will react against him in earth changes, earthquakes, storms and floods. On the deeper level we must recognize that our own wrong-doing and faulty thinking is a factor in causing these great disturbances which threaten us.

If mankind is to survive as a species, he must learn to work with Gaia, the goddess of earth. The human race, integrally part of

147

nature, is an aspect of the consciousness of the living being of the planet. At present industrial man is 'bleeding' the earth of her living energy and heat by massive entropy (*see* Kit Pedler's remarkable book 'The Quest for Gaia'). The alternative life-style now emerging on a wide front represents the many movements working for conservation, for harmony of all life and for a new society based not on competition and violence but on co-operation. To take part in these activities calls for a love of nature and a feeling for the kinship with all life as a great Oneness working in harmony. If in addition we are drawn to the great holistic concepts of the spiritual nature of man and the universe, we shall see that the New Pilgrimage is a vital factor in the very salvation of the earth. We are making a constructive contribution to the cleansing and depolluting of the planet. Since human free will must always be respected by the angelic beings in their operation for redemption of the planet, we may feel that conscious pilgrimage amounts to a form of invocation and prayer, attuning to the higher worlds and inviting the inflooding of the forces of light. It serves a vital function in the coming time of change. Bunyan's great hymn takes on greater meaning for us.

> He who would valiant be
> Gainst all disaster.
> Let him in constancy
> Follow the Master.
> There's no discouragement
> Will make him once relent.
> His first, avowed intent
> To be a Pilgrim.